Nana's *Gift*

A Recipe for
Mind, Body, and Spirit

Rev. Leslie Lopes Foster

Published by Hollace House Publishing Spokane Valley, Washington

Nana's Gift: A Recipe for Mind, Body, and Spirit
Copyright 2023 Leslie Lopes Foster

Scripture quotations taken from The Holy Bible, New International Version® NIV® Copyright © 1973, 1978, 1984, 2011 by Biblica, Inc.
Used with permission. All rights reserved worldwide.

For more information or to contact the author: lesliefoster138@gmail.com

Book cover design: Christine Dupre, www.vidagraphicdesign.com
Book design: Russ Davis, Gray Dog Press, www.graydogpress.com
Book editing: Barbara Hollace, www.barbarahollace.com

Photography credit (author's photo): Erica Carryl, Vine and Branch Photography
www.vineandbranchphoto.com

Photography credit (historical family photos): Family photo albums

ISBN: 979-8-9854092-2-2

Printed in the United States of America

To Todd,

My husband, my hero, my heart.
Your encouragement and support have been immeasurable.

Acknowledgments

I would like to thank my wonderful children Erica Carryl, Stefanie Brown, and Jeremy Brown who afforded me the honor of becoming a nana. My daughters have cheered and supported me through this entire writing journey. Their constructive feedback has been invaluable. I want to acknowledge my sons-in-law, Dwain Carryl and Eli Brown, who are loving husbands to my daughters and fantastic fathers to my grandchildren. I also want to thank my daughter-in-law, Lindsay Brown, an incredible mom to my three other grandchildren.

Thank you, Pat Cross, my dear friend, for often reading through my raw writings and providing invaluable input. Thank you for your support in taking this journey with me.

I also want to acknowledge the many women who prayed me through this journey. You were always there to offer a word of encouragement. I am grateful to you.

Sheri Powell, my dear sister, your suggestions certainly enhanced this project. God bless you for connecting me with the most gifted editing/publishing team of Barbara Hollace, Christine Dupre, and Russ Davis.

Thank you Barb, Christine, and Russ.

Thank you to my eight wonderful grandchildren, Luke, Chase, Jaylem, Karis, Makena, Gracelynn, Sage, and Sophia. My love for you is on every page of this work. You have been a gift to me. This book is my gift to you. Thank you for always inspiring me to embrace new opportunities and view this world through a hopeful lens.

Most of all, I acknowledge my Lord and Savior, Jesus Christ. I pray that you Lord, above all, find these writings to be pleasing in Your sight.

Contents

RELATIONAL LIFE LESSONS

Introduction

The table is set. The meal is about to be served. I invite you to come, take your seat and dine. Nana's Gift is a recipe for the mind, body, and spirit! It's not meant to be comfort food for you to partake of alone in front of a TV. It is intended for parents or grandparents and teens to literally sit around a table and learn from one another.

It was written as an aid to help my grandchildren walk a productive Christ-centered life and to some day pass along their own spiritual legacy. But, as I share my heart with my family, I also welcome you to my table. We might not share the same biological DNA, but our connection to our heavenly Father makes us family. It is my desire that all who read this book will be able to grasp helpful nuggets and perhaps replicate that which is good. The examples shared come from the Bible, my life, and the lives of those dearest to me. The book addresses topics from "how to handle money" to "how to choose the right spouse" and everything in between! Although the book is biblically based, it offers simple practical life advice. When appropriate, I used my own family as examples, to give my grandchildren a sense of where and from whom they come. Hopefully they will embrace this book as "my legacy of love."

My prayer is that you and your loved ones will also be inspired to take pride in your family of origin and perhaps even have some healthy dialogue around some of the topics presented. Each section ends with three "Table Talk Questions" to help initiate intimate family conversations. Nana's Gift also contains some of our family's favorite recipes. The book truly is "a recipe for the mind, body, and spirit." May your walk with the Lord and your relationship with your family be nourished and strengthened as you too "unwrap" Nana's Gift.

SPIRITUAL LIFE LESSONS

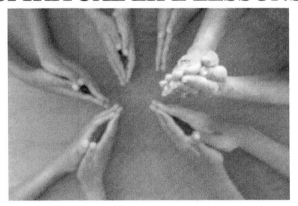

1

Salvation: Nana's Wish for You

A personal relationship with Christ will transform your life
by adding both purpose and destiny

*For God so loved the world that He gave His one and only Son, that whoever
believes in Him shall not perish but have eternal life. —John 3:16*

When we bring bananas home from the supermarket, they are often more green than yellow. If we let them sit too long, they turn from green, to yellow, to brown. They are not thrown out; we merely find a new purpose for them. Brown bananas are perfect for making banana bread.

As an eight-year-old child, banana bread was the first recipe I made by myself. I had much practice as Nannie appointed me to be the unofficial brown banana smasher of the family.

When we accept Jesus as our savior, God says that we become new creations in Christ. Just like those brown bananas, we find new purpose, new potential, and new possibilities. There is a recipe for delicious banana bread in the appendix. Make it, enjoy it, and thank God for brown bananas. Consider how wonderful they were in fulfilling a new purpose, potential, and possibilities. Think about how wonderful you will be when God does the same with you!

Recipe #1: Banana Bread (pg. 138)

My Dear Grandchildren,

More than anything, my prayer is for each of you to come into a personal relationship with Christ. Every one of us was born with a God-shaped "hole" in our souls only He can fill. Many people go through life sensing something deep within them is missing, but unfortunately, they look in all the wrong places to fill the void. Only Jesus can satisfy the craving of an empty soul.

Throughout my life, I have watched those who did not know Christ live their lives the best way they knew how. Unfortunately, their lives became a pursuit to fill the "hole" in their soul with things such as money, drugs, alcohol, worldly success, and other things that only left them empty and still searching. None of the things they pursued were able to bring the peace and abundant life only Jesus can provide. The things of the world bring temporary satisfaction, but ultimately, those without Christ are left empty and unfulfilled.

Everyone is born separated from our holy God because of our sin nature. We all need the cleansing Christ provided by shedding His blood on the cross, dying, and then rising again in the power of the resurrection. And yet, no one is too sinful to be outside the reach of God's love. He wants a personal relationship with everyone. Nana and Grandad want you to experience the richness of having a relationship with Christ. Our lives have no eternal substance or meaning without the spirit of Christ living with us and through us.

Having received Jesus at sixteen made a profound difference in my life. Until the age of twelve, Nana attended a Catholic Church with her grandmother, Linda Fermino Lopes, Papa's mother. The church service was often in Latin, and I really didn't understand much. However, it was in that Catholic Church where the importance of reverencing and respecting God was first instilled in me. Your great-great-grandmother, Nana Lopes was Catholic all the days of her life and clearly loved Jesus with all her heart. She had a very real personal relationship with Him, and consequently was a great spiritual influence in my life.

At the age of sixteen, both my best friend (Auntie Kathy) and a cousin of mine (who had been one of those who previously looked in all the wrong places for peace), invited me to a special service at the church they had been attending. It was a Nazarene church in the city of New Bedford, Massachusetts led by a Cape Verdean pastor named Rev. Manuel Chavier.

This Nazarene Church was different from the Catholic Church I attended growing up. It was different in the sense that everything was understandable (it was in English), and the pastor taught directly out of the Bible. The people were friendly, loving, and possessed a strong sense of community.

When attending the Nazarene Church, peace saturated my spirit. In a matter of months after listening to Pastor Chavier's sermons, I decided to confess my sins, open my heart to Jesus, and ask Him to be Lord over my life. Following me down the aisle to say "yes" to Jesus on that precious day were my mother (Nannie) and brother (Uncle Carl). Praise God, what a wonderful day it was for all of us!

Receiving Christ has been by far my best decision ever. It truly transformed and redirected my life. Because of this one decision, "to live for Christ," my life has been filled with much peace and joy, even in the midst of difficult times. That "hole" in my soul was healed by the Holy Spirit who now lives within me. I am never alone. God is always guiding and directing me. No other decision in my life has been more important. That one decision also settled the question as to where I would spend eternity. I never have to wonder what will become of me when life as I know it comes to an end. I will not spend a godless eternity. Instead, I will dwell in His presence forever. I desire the same richness of life, both now and throughout eternity for you, my grandchildren.

There will be many "imitations" of God that will call to you but be wise enough to reject them and embrace the only one who has the power to heal, guide, save, and direct you. "Jesus is the way, the truth and the life" (John14:6) now and forever. My prayer is that you will grab hold of Jesus' hand today. It is as easy as saying a quiet prayer and sincerely asking Him for the forgiveness of your sins. Then ask Him to come into your heart as Lord and Savior. My heart's desire is that my grandchildren receive Christ and allow Him to lead them all the days of their lives.

"If you declare with your mouth, 'Jesus is Lord,' and believe in your heart that God raised him from the dead, you will be saved. For it is with your heart that you believe and are justified, and with your mouth that you profess your faith and are saved." (Romans 10:9-10)

May you choose to walk with Jesus.

All my love,
Nana

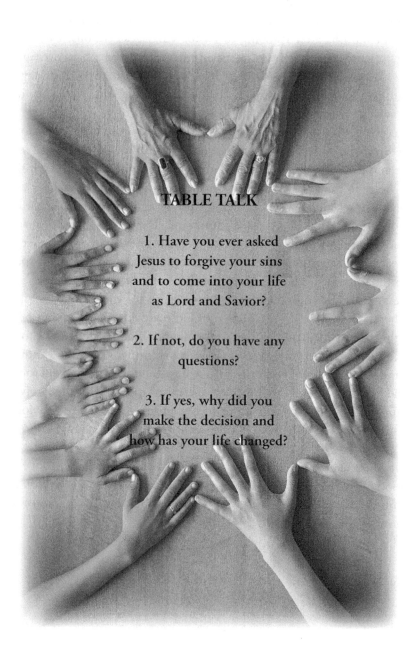

TABLE TALK

1. Have you ever asked Jesus to forgive your sins and to come into your life as Lord and Savior?

2. If not, do you have any questions?

3. If yes, why did you make the decision and how has your life changed?

2

Know Who You Are in Christ

Only God has the right to define who you are and who He
has created you to be

For you created my inmost being; you knit me together in my mother's womb.
I praise you because I am fearfully and wonderfully made; your works are
wonderful, I know that full well. —Psalm 139:13-14

Sometimes at our family birthday celebrations, we sit around the table with
a birthday cake adorned with candles as the centerpiece. Everyone shares
one thing we love about the guest of honor. It's human nature to want to be
accepted and affirmed within our families and beyond. Our first impressions
of ourselves come from the words and sentiments of those who love us and
know us best. And yet, there is no one who loves us or knows us quite as fully
as God. It's important we take the time to find out who He says we are. After
all, we are His design and creation.

Today's recipe is mandarin orange cake, one of our family favorites.
It has many ingredients and each one contributes to a delicious, finished
product. You are one of God's recipes. All of your life experiences will be used
as ingredients to make you one of His favorites! Nothing in or about you is
by accident. God knew what He was doing when He created you. Accept
yourself. Love yourself. Live as He uniquely created you to be.

Recipe #2: Mandarin Orange Cake (pg. 138)

My Dear Grandchildren,

One of the more important pursuits in your life is to discover who God has uniquely made you to be. This is no easy task. It begins the moment you ask God into your heart and His Holy Spirit comes to reside in you. That simple act will initiate a lifelong relationship of seeking, submitting to, and following God. If you completely surrender to Him, the Holy Spirit will become your closest friend—guiding, directing, and leading you. God has created and filled you with all the ingredients that will enable you to effectively walk out His plans for your life. It's important to come to recognize those ingredients and develop them fully. Start with a desire to walk in the fullness of His plans.

Take the time to know and appreciate who you are in Christ. If you don't do so, others may try to define you by speaking words and expressing intentions over you that God never intended. They have neither the right nor the authority to do so. The only expectations you need to be concerned about are those of your creator. Let His expectations become your personal desires. When your goals are in harmony with His, He will partner with you to bring them to pass. Reject any negative comments, labels, or images others say about you. Let what God says about you BE the words you carry in your heart. Remember who you are and to whom you belong. You belong to the King of kings—God Himself. Love who He has made you to be and embrace His goodness inside of you.

Get to know what you like and dislike, what you do well and not so well. Celebrate and operate out of your strengths; give more attention to your strengths than your weaknesses. When you work out of your strengths, it builds confidence, enabling you to boldly walk in God's ordained plans. Yes, we must work on our weaknesses, but we must work OUT of our strengths. Think about what brings you joy. Give thought to what you are passionate about. These are all clues to discovering yourself and once discovered, they will provide you with a divine compass to direct you throughout your life. There is only one you on this earth. Just "do you." You are wonderfully and fearfully made (Psalm 139:14). Be yourself, your BEST self, and watch how God will use you to make a difference in this world.

Nana and Grandad love you dearly.

All my love,
Nana

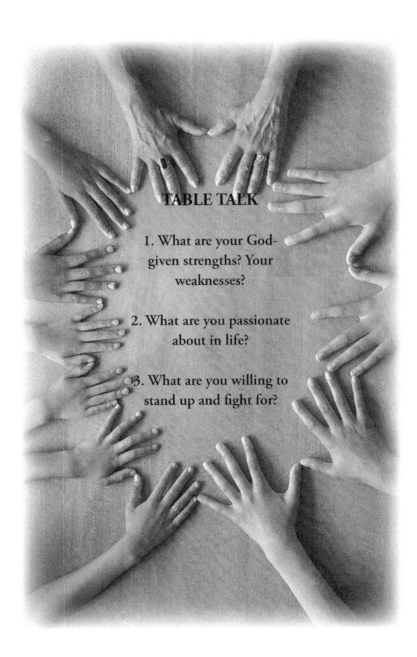

TABLE TALK

1. What are your God-given strengths? Your weaknesses?

2. What are you passionate about in life?

3. What are you willing to stand up and fight for?

3

Walk in Humility

God delights in those who walk humbly before Him in
obedience

Humility is the fear of the Lord; its wages are riches and honor and life.
—Proverbs 22:4

The dinner table can serve as a great place for confessions. Whatever
else is being served, sometimes there needs to be some "humble pie"
on the menu. When we need to admit that we were wrong and ask for
forgiveness in a matter, it's called "eating humble pie." Often, it can be the
best part of the meal. It leads to healing and deepens relationships. Mom
and Dad don't always get everything right. Neither do children. Words
like, "I was wrong" and "I'm sorry" go a long way in the making of strong
families. There's no humble pie in our recipe box, but we do have a simple,
delicious key lime pie to offer.

Recipe #3: Key Lime Pie (pg. 139)

My Dear Grandchildren,

Humility is a character trait that is often undervalued and disregarded in our society. In the Bible, humility is considered a key element to living a successful Christian life. A person who possesses humility is one who has a modest opinion of their own importance. A humble person does not think more highly of themselves than they ought. (Romans 12:3). Unfortunately, we live in a day where many people esteem themselves far too much. They have believed their own prideful opinions and have subsequently elevated themselves above others, and often, even the Lord Himself. Having confidence is necessary, but at the point we begin to think more highly of ourselves than others, we have fallen into pride. By His grace, God made us "good," but we are never to think of ourselves as "better" than anyone.

Whenever we ignore the Lord's directions or outright disobey His commands, we place ourselves above Him. Such behavior displays an absence of humility and the presence of pride. "God opposes the proud but gives grace to the humble." (James 4:6)

Beloved grandchildren, know that you have been fashioned and created by God. He remains the one we worship, submit to, and follow. The word of God says, "to have humility is to fear the Lord." Always keep God in His rightful place in both your heart and mind. He is Lord and we are His servants. We are not His equal, nor are we in control of our lives. It is God who brings every good thing to us and sees that all our needs are met. It is God who opens doors of opportunity and closes doors that are not meant for us to go through. It is He who bestows the talents and gifts we possess, and it is God who can very easily take them away.

I encourage you to honor the Lord and give Him His due respect. Acknowledge and include God in everything you do and give Him praise in your accomplishments. Only He deserves all glory. Without God, we can do nothing of significance. Proverbs 22:4 says if we possess "humility" we will gain riches, honor, and life. We don't have to strive and fight our way through life. We need only to display humility by fearing the Lord. Fearing the Lord can take on many different forms, but it always has one common denominator, obedience. When we obey, we demonstrate our hearts are submitted to God's will and lordship. We display fear and honor of the Lord when we obey His commandments, His Word, and His voice as brought forth by the Holy Spirit. God loves and delights in a humble heart.

Proverbs 8:32-35 says, "Now then, my children, listen to me; Blessed are those who keep my ways. Listen to my instruction and be wise; Do not disregard it. Blessed are those who listen to me, watching daily at my doors. Waiting at my doorway. For those who find me find life and receive favor from the Lord."

God's counsel should take precedence over any other counsel. A person who walks in humility inwardly concedes their great need for God. Proverbs 8 tells us that when we listen and heed God's counsel, we will find favor. Strive to walk in humility and watch what God will do. It will be exceedingly, abundantly, more than you can think or ask. Do not get puffed up and full of yourself like many in the world. Instead walk in humility, positioning yourself to experience the "goodness of the Lord in the land of the living." (Psalm 27:13)

Use your "goodness", skills, and resources to help improve the lives of other human beings and God will take care of you in extraordinary ways. Displaying this kind of behavior toward others is what it means to count them as more significant than yourselves. This kind of humility wins God's favor.

All my love,
Nana

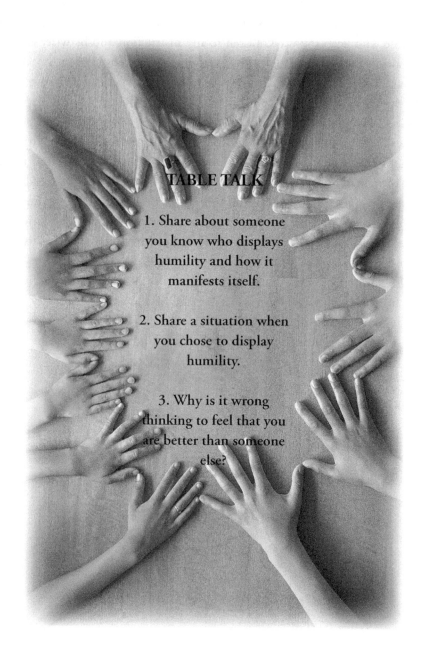

TABLE TALK

1. Share about someone you know who displays humility and how it manifests itself.

2. Share a situation when you chose to display humility.

3. Why is it wrong thinking to feel that you are better than someone else?

4

See Your Future Through God's Eyes

May you see beyond your natural eye and embrace God's
vision for your life

*Then the Lord replied: "Write down the revelation make it plain on tablets so
that a herald may run with it. For the revelation awaits an appointed time; it
speaks of the end and will not prove false. Though it linger, wait for it; it will
certainly come and will not delay." —Habakkuk 2:2-3*

As a second grader, my teacher asked each student to share one of their
favorite food dishes. I decided to share about the Cape Verdean stew-
like dish called Manchup (pronounced: mon-'choop). I told my teacher Mrs.
Lawee the dish was made with bird food (samp/hominy), leaves (bay leaves),
beans, and grass (kale). Bird food, leaves, and grass. That is the way my seven-
year-old eyes saw it. There will be times when others fail to see what we
see. My teacher was so concerned about my family's financial well-being she
called our home that evening to see how she could help.

Nannie was not too happy with me and asked that I not share family
business with outsiders. From my seven-year-old perspective, what I shared
was accurate. Manchup is made differently from island to island in Cape
Verde, but one thing all Cape Verdeans can probably agree on is that it is a
comfort food. To this day, Manchup is still one of my favorite dishes.

Recipe #4: Nannie's Manchup (aka Cachupa) (pg. 140)

My Dear Grandchildren,

My prayer is that each of my grandchildren will always possess clear vision. I'm talking about the God-given vision for your future He will place in your heart. May each of you be able to clearly see what will only be possible with God on your side and faith in your hearts. These big, God-sized dreams will require big, God-sized help. Trust Him to bring forth both empowerment from above and encouragement here below. We all need encouragement.

Once you have God's vision, keep moving toward it. Do not be discouraged if other people don't understand or believe in you, keep your focus on Jesus every step of the way. It will be God who will accomplish the vision through you. It doesn't matter if what He has shown you has never been done before. If the vision is from God, know that He can bring it to pass. You must do your part and be obedient to follow Him. God will do the rest. Pray that you'll be able to see what God sees. He sees past circumstances, situations, and people as they are now and what they can become with His help.

The first person in my life who helped impart vision and encourage me was my second-grade teacher, Mrs. Thelma Lawee. I wouldn't say she was my best teacher, but she was amazingly inspirational. Mrs. Lawee believed in her little second grade class of Cape Verdean children. She told us that we were as important as the president of the United States, who back in 1962 was President John F. Kennedy. As a second grader my thought was, "Wow, I really am important, I am somebody." In that class, I made the decision to become like Mrs. Lawee, a teacher who encouraged all children to see their importance and reach their potential.

Eugenia "Jan" Lopes

The second person who influenced and created vision in my life was my own mother "Jan" Lopes, known to you as Nannie. Nannie always had a vision of living a better life. From the time I was four years old, Nannie birthed a desire in my heart to go to college. Even though we knew very few people who had attended college, Nannie instilled in her children the merit of a good education which would enable us to succeed in life. She also talked my dad into

16

moving to the suburbs, an unfortunate necessity for us to be able to receive a better education than was available in the city.

It was Nannie who went to bat for me when I graduated from high school and wanted to attend a private women's college in Boston. This was something my father thought was too expensive and not necessary. Nannie convinced Papa that going to college in Boston would expose me to greater opportunities and introduce me to new and interesting people. Without Nannie's vision for a better life for her children, my life would have turned out quite differently. I would have never met Grandad, never traveled out of the country, and probably never become a teacher or co-pastor. Nannie was a mother who had dreams and vision for her children's lives, and for that I'm grateful. She taught me to think and believe—"I can do all things through Christ who strengthens me." (Philippians 4:13)

Dear grandchildren, walk out the dreams God places in your spirit. Know your Nana and Grandad will be right beside you singing and cheering you on. Go Luke the Duke! Go Chay Chay! Go Jay Jay! Go Kay Kay! Go Mak Mak! Go Gracie! Go Say Say! Go Sophie! You can do it! Believe in the God who is in you.

All my love,
Nana

TABLE TALK

1. What is a dream/vision God has placed in your heart to be accomplished with His help?

2. Why does it seem impossible?

3. How can we be supportive to our family and friends as they pursue their dreams?

5

Rise Up and Fight

Battles are won and lost according to what we believe

"And we know that in all things God works for the good of those who love him, who have been called according to his purpose." —Romans 8:28

Despite the many occasions they argued and fought (as siblings are prone to do), Grandad knew his older brother really loved him. It became clear the day his brother warded off a threatening older kid…at the cost of getting beat up himself!

Protection comes in many forms. In families, it can be a watchful parent or an older sibling who does the protecting. In nature, protection can be as simple as a God-given shell surrounding a tasty nut. Anyone who has cracked open a nut to get to the tender morsel inside knows how well-protected it is.

God is our ultimate protector. Sometimes, our trust and confidence in Him acts as a protective shell around us, warding off the lies and worst intentions of the Devil. Today's note provides just such an account.

In my Pistachio Nut Cake recipe, you'll be glad to know there are no nuts to crack open. The flavor comes from the pudding and not actual nuts. Try it! Grandad jokingly says this cake was the reason he married me. He loves it, but thankfully, he loves me more.

Recipe #5: Pistachio Nut Cake (pg.141)

My Dear Grandchildren,

We are in a spiritual war. You need to be prepared to fight it God's way. As you choose to walk in the rich Christian heritage at the center of our family, you will realize there is an enemy who has declared war against you. Our walk with God threatens the dark spirits of this world.

Just as surely as there is a God in heaven, there is an evil spirit named Satan whose job it is to steal, kill, and ultimately destroy the children of God (John 10:10). It is very important we learn how to fight against the devil's schemes. The battle is real, but the Bible gives us a pathway to victory.

Nothing brought the concept of God's protection closer to home than the battle fought for my own father's life. Papa (Jeppy Lopes) was 78 years old when he underwent knee replacement surgery. Having traveled to Massachusetts to be by his side for the operation, the doctors' assessment was everything went well. Shortly after the surgery, we were able to converse with Papa. Believing he was on the road to recovery, I headed back home to Connecticut to finish preparing to host our annual women's church conference.

One evening during the conference while praying for people, my spirit was jarred by these words, "I'm going to kill your father!" There was no doubt in my mind that these words came directly from Satan.

After praying for multiple women, I proceeded to my room only to receive a phone call from Nannie telling me Papa had taken a turn for the worse and it didn't look good. After reassuring Nannie of my intention to return to Massachusetts as soon as the conference ended, a group of us began to intercede for Papa. Upon my return to his bedside, Papa was in a coma and the doctors were suggesting our family members be called in to say their goodbyes.

With very few medical options left, we asked the doctors to remove Papa from all medications, which they did. However, he remained comatose as his health declined rapidly. All we could do was pray. During one of my personal prayer times, feeling impressed to ask God if this was Papa's time to die—I clearly heard the answer, "No." With this assurance, we began to wage war in prayer with everything we had.

A call for spiritual reinforcements brought two dear friends from Connecticut to join me in prayer at Papa's bedside. They came up on a Friday evening and the three of us prayed over Papa for about an hour. At that point we felt at peace, extended our faith to believe for the very best, and left the hospital to spend the night in my childhood home.

The next morning, just before 7:00 am, Nannie answered a call on the kitchen phone. It was the hospital. Hearing the phone ring but fearing the worst, I stayed in bed straining to hear my mother's side of the conversation. Nannie let out a shriek and my heart sank. No matter how prepared we think we are to receive bad news, it's still hard to face when it actually comes.

As it turned out, the phone call was good news, not the bad news we all feared. The hospital called to let us know Papa had come out of the coma and was asking for something to eat. Praise God! God's miraculous, healing hand had moved on our behalf. Papa went on to see another granddaughter and grandson get married and to welcome three great-grandchildren into the world. We could easily have accepted the lie of the devil and just waited for Papa to die. Instead, we chose to believe God and put our faith in Him for the outcome. God protected my father from what would have been a premature death, but it was our faith, our trust in what we felt that He was saying to us, and our refusal to give up and give in that turned the situation around. The devil is a liar. Do not ever forget that, dear ones. If God had decided to take my dad home at that time, we would have had to accept His will, but it was not His will. The whole experience became a great lesson in the power of God moving through the exercised gift of faith. It all worked together for good, and for that I will be forever grateful.

Do not believe every negative thing you see or hear. Find out what God has to say and dare to take Him at His word. He is still the God of the miraculous!

All my love,
Nana

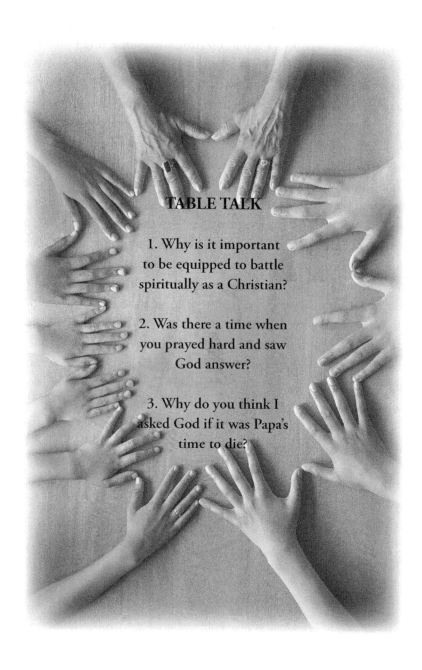

TABLE TALK

1. Why is it important to be equipped to battle spiritually as a Christian?

2. Was there a time when you prayed hard and saw God answer?

3. Why do you think I asked God if it was Papa's time to die?

6

Keep Yourself Holy, Part 1 (The Problem)

Be intentional in keeping yourself physically and spiritually wholesome to honor God

Don't you know that you yourselves are God's temple and that God's Spirit dwells in your midst? . . .God's temple is sacred, and you together are that temple. —1 Corinthians 3:16-17

Luke, our first-born grandchild, was just shy of his third birthday when one Thanksgiving his mom dished toddler-sized portions of turkey and traditional holiday foods onto his plate. We were taken aback when he started crying real tears and pointed toward the door screaming, "Toochies!"

At the age of two, turkey wasn't Luke's idea of a great meal. Bertucci's was the name of his favorite pizza restaurant and THAT is what he wanted. Who doesn't love a good pizza? And yet, sometimes we need to make healthier choices for our minds, bodies, and souls. This lesson, in two parts, deals with making healthy and holy choices pertaining to our bodies.

You'll find a good healthy recipe for "Canja" Cape Verdean chicken soup. Recipe #6: Canja (Cape Verdean Chicken Soup) (pg. 142)

My Dear Grandchildren,

My desire is for you to reap the benefits of a righteously lived life. Our bodies were created by God to carry His presence here on earth. They were made to worship and honor Him, and not primarily for our own pleasure. I'll tell you the truth, dear ones. It's easier said than done to keep our bodies holy and in line with their divine purpose. Everywhere we turn, there are persuasive voices trying to convince us to use and abuse our bodies in ways that are displeasing to God. You will be enticed and encouraged to explore unwholesome sinful avenues. My dear precious grandchildren, people will not only encourage you to participate in unholy things; they will try to make you feel there is something wrong with you if you don't!

Even if their voices were silenced, the inner cravings of our own flesh fight against God and try to take us out of His will. It's a battle that I want you to be aware of. Temptations come to us all. Half of the battle is being aware that you will be tempted and preparing yourself for when it comes. The other half is knowing what to do when it happens.

There are several areas of temptation when it comes to our bodies. Let's look at them:

Food temptations: Food is the fuel we need to keep our bodies going. We can't exist without the nourishment food provides. God has made eating a pleasurable experience for most of us with healthy appetites. There are very few people I know who don't like to eat. But if we become more concerned with the pleasure of eating than the nutritional necessity of eating, the results can become disastrous. While food was meant to keep us healthy and strong, the abuse of food in pursuit of pleasure can make us sick, weak, obese, and lead to premature death. We need to be mindful to eat healthy, balanced diets and use moderation in choosing what and how much we eat. We must "eat to live" and not "live to eat." In recent years, obesity (i.e., a disease that results in excessive body fat) has grown in epic proportions, making many quite unhealthy and often leaving people unable to fulfill God's plans for their lives.

Sometimes obesity is the result of a food addiction. People try to comfort themselves with food rather than learning how the Word of God can be a great source of peace and guidance. God sees addictive behaviors as strongholds from which we must be set free. We don't have to be obese to have food working against us rather than for us. The wrong kinds of foods are harmful in and of themselves. Too much fried food, processed food, and sweets take a toll on our bodies. When we combine poor food choices with a lack of proper exercise, we're talking about a lifestyle that can literally kill you.

Sexual temptations: When we yield to sexual temptation, it leads to sexual immorality. Sexual immorality occurs when a person has sex with someone with whom they are not married. God created sex for married couples to strengthen and affirm their oneness and create babies. By having sex outside of marriage, we become one with someone whom God never intended us to be intimate. When we become physically intimate with someone, their spirit becomes one with our spirit. Sex is not just a physical act, but a very spiritual act. God created sex as a point of intimacy between a husband and a wife, not as a recreational activity to be indulged in with just anyone. God wants us to respect and value our bodies and live in a way that acknowledges His very spirit lives within us.

In pastoring, Grandad and Nana have had the opportunity to counsel many married couples. The couples who seemed happiest and most satisfied in their married lives were the ones who tried to honor God in all their ways.

Alcohol and Drug temptations: Alcohol and drugs are used by many to alter their mental state. Marijuana and alcohol may be legal in many places today, but that doesn't mean they are good for you. The apostle Paul said, "I have the right to do anything," you say—but not everything is beneficial. "I have the right to do anything"—but not everything is constructive. (1 Corinthians 10:23).

Drug and alcohol use may bring temporary pleasure, but they often carry lifetime consequences. No one ever sets out or chooses to become a drug addict, or an alcoholic, but it happens far too often. For some people, all it took was "one time" and their lives were changed forever. You also need to know that some families, as well as some individuals, are more prone to these vices and become more easily hooked than others. You have no way of knowing if you will be more susceptible. I urge you to stay away from such vices. Satan likes nothing more than to entrap one of God's saints and then ruin their lives. We have people in our family who have struggled all their lives because of these bondages. I do not want you to become one of them.

All my love,
Nana

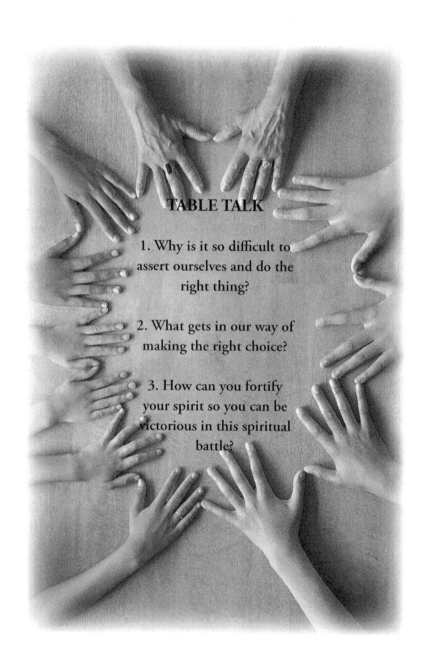

TABLE TALK

1. Why is it so difficult to assert ourselves and do the right thing?

2. What gets in our way of making the right choice?

3. How can you fortify your spirit so you can be victorious in this spiritual battle?

7

Keep Yourself Holy, Part 2, (The Solution)

Do not explore sinful avenues but keep your body as a holy,
living sacrifice to God.

Finally, my brethren, be strong in the Lord, and in the power of his might.
—Ephesians 6:10

During my childhood, the family frying pan got quite a bit of use. It was an easy meal and what came out of it sure did taste good. Hamburgers, pork chops, chicken, fish, and even Spam (look it up!) all went from the frying pan to the dinner plate on a regular basis. For a double whammy of fried AND processed food, fried bologna was not uncommon. Fried foods fall within a broader category of less than healthy eating referred to by nutritionists as SAD, or the Standard American Diet.

We're making wiser choices these days. We're eating more salads, fruits, and vegetables, and less fried foods, processed meats, and sugar-sweetened beverages. We're trying to be kinder to our bodies with the hope they will last longer and serve us better over time.

While the recipe in the appendix for basic marinated carrots may not get an A-rating from health food advocates, it's a far cry better for you than say, fried bologna. Living a life that is pleasing to God is all about the choices we make on a daily basis and determining to find strength in the Lord to resist temptation.

Recipe #7: Marinated Carrots (pg. 143)

My Dear Grandchildren,

We will always have temptations to deal with in our lives. It's very easy for me to suggest that you should just make the right choices and resist temptation. The truth is making the right decisions in the face of temptation will require a strength that is greater than our own. We need God's help and His strength to do the right thing. Our opening verse quoted the apostle Paul, ". . . be strong in the Lord and in the power of his might." How do we become strong in the Lord?

Read the Word of God. In Psalm 119:11, the psalmist said, "I have hidden your word in my heart that I might not sin against you." The more you read your Bible and memorize scripture, the more your thoughts and even your desires will line up with God's desires for you. Just as the body needs food in order to be strong, your soul and spirit need the Word of God to gain strength and prevail over our competing desires to commit sin.

Pray: In Luke 22:40, Jesus said, "Pray that you will not fall into temptation." Prayer is what keeps us in tune with God. It's the means of communication whereby we speak with God and God speaks with us. If we do not have an active prayer life, we'll be influenced by everything and everyone except the one who matters most! Prayer, like reading the Bible, is a spiritual exercise that will keep you strong when temptation comes.

Think: Without question, our friends, peers, and modern culture will influence how we act and even the clothes we wear. The influence of others can range from absolutely harmless to potentially deadly. 1 Corinthians 15:33 reads, "Do not be misled: 'Bad company corrupts good character.'" All I am suggesting is that you think through the choices you make and don't simply go along with the crowd by using the excuse, "Everybody's doing it!"

Over the years, many fashion trends have come and gone. Back when Grandad and I were teenagers, the fashion and cultural fad was to wear our hair in an Afro, a big natural hairdo appearing to add several inches to our height. The bigger the Afro, the better. I sported a very large one. My mother (Nannie) would often say to me, "You look ridiculous!" My hair was making a statement that I do not regret making, but from the perspective of my mother's generation, I understand how she must have felt. It's okay to make a conscious decision others may not agree with, but make sure your decision comes at the end of a thought process, rather than just the blind following of others. The look we adopt for ourselves makes a statement to the world. "Others are doing it" is never a sufficient reason to do something. Think.

Our appearance should be a true reflection of ourselves without dishonoring God in the process. Be wise with the fads and fashions you choose to follow. Give thought to the fads that will be permanent, like tattoos and face piercings that cannot be undone. In the Old Testament, these two fads were methods used to mark one's slaves. Think.

Elegant brides have walked self-consciously down the aisle on their wedding day because of their tattoos. Ask yourself, "Is this dishonoring God and the body He created?" Regretfully, some young people will enter their elderly years with wrinkled tattoos on wrinkled bodies. Be mindful and wise as to what you do to your "temple"; it belongs to God. Think.

Be modest. What does it say about you to everyone you meet when your clothes are too tight, too revealing, and too sexy? Is this the message you really want to convey? Is it the first impression you really want to make? I'll say it one more time, just because I love you, think!

All my love,
Nana

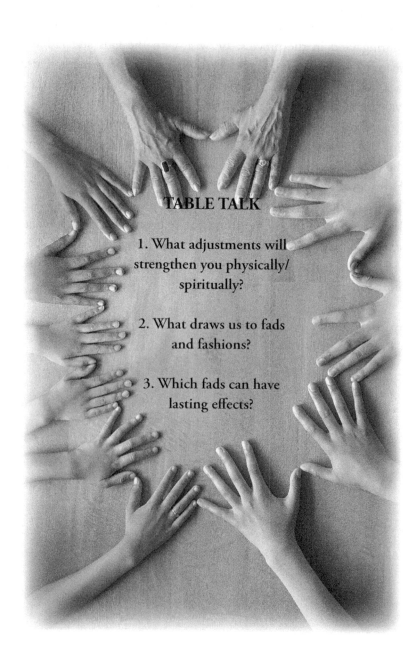

TABLE TALK

1. What adjustments will strengthen you physically/ spiritually?

2. What draws us to fads and fashions?

3. Which fads can have lasting effects?

8

Fear vs. Faith

Confronting and overcoming fear with God's equipping
and empowering Holy Spirit

*So do not fear, for I am with you; Do not be dismayed, for I am your God. I
will strengthen you and help you: I will uphold you with my righteous right
hand. —Isaiah 41:10*

Several years ago, Grandad and I spent a week in Costa Rica with my
brother, Carl and his wife, Kathy. When Grandad and I were assigned to
a ground level room, it was not my preference. But we accepted it. . . until
I noticed creatures resembling a cross between rats, monkeys, and raccoons
traveling in large packs all around the premises. They called them coatis
(pronounced Ko-wah'-tees). No thanks! I was scared of them and insisted on
being moved. Fortunately, Uncle Carl and Aunt Kathy let us switch rooms for
their second-floor unit. Much to my embarrassment, coatis are quite harmless
and very interesting to watch. There was no good reason for me to be afraid
of them, but I was.

Sometimes we get "chicken" for no good reason. Today's recipe, Chicken
Divan, is one of my favorites to serve to company.
Recipe #8: Chicken Divan (pg. 143)

My Dear Grandchildren,

In life, you'll find that fear is one of the greatest roadblocks you'll face while attempting to walk out God's plans and purposes. The dictionary definition of "fear" is "a distressing emotion aroused by impending danger, evil, or pain whether the threat is real or imagined." Although "fear" is a short word in the English language, it can wield much power if not confronted. And yet, throughout the Bible, God exhorts us to overcome fear. What is important for us to understand is that fear is a God-given emotion meant to protect us from danger, not to imprison or keep us from our destiny.

How can we acknowledge our fears without giving in to them? At some point in your lives, you will face situations or circumstances (whether real or imagined) that will make you fearful. To achieve all God has intended for your life, it will be necessary for you to learn how to conquer your fears. From my own experience, I have learned that my imagination often exaggerates situations, making them far more threatening than they really are. Typically, nothing is as bad as my mind and emotions make it out to be.

When you are feeling fearful, ask God to give you a clear and accurate picture of the situation. What's really the worst that can happen? Once you can accurately see the situation from God's perspective, ask Him for the strength, wisdom, and courage to deal with it. Stick to the truth and move forward, trusting God to see you through.

Your Nana considers herself to be a friendly but reserved person. Having never been fond of public speaking, the mere thought of standing in front of an audience used to terrify me. As God would have it, I ended up in ministry speaking before hundreds. While I can't say I ever enjoyed it, I learned to confront my fear and lean into God to accomplish what He desired to do through me. The feedback I received from others was often very encouraging. With God's help, fear gave way to confidence.

In walking with God for many years, learning to nourish and fortify my spirit with His Word has been key. I've learned to strengthen my spirit with the Word of God to shut the mouth of the voice of fear by repeating to myself verses like, ". . . in all these things we are more than conquerors through him who loved us" (Romans 8:37).

"No weapon forged against you will prevail" (Isaiah 54:17). "I can do all this through him who gives me strength" (Philippians 4:13).

If you let him, the devil will try to taunt and bully you until you're all but paralyzed with fear. When attacked in such a manner, our focus must be on God and His Word. We can only overcome if we know, believe, and stand upon God's Word. It is in these moments that God through the Holy Spirit has the power to transform our fear into the confidence we call faith. The transfer of power from fear to faith makes a way for us to walk in the victory God has intended for our lives.

My dear grandchildren, never let fear overcome you. Remember God created fear to protect, not shackle us. I've watched far too many people live small, seemingly safe lives, confined and contained within the prison walls of their unreasonable fears. There is no safer place than being in God's will. Each time you confront and conquer your fears, it strengthens your faith and gives you more boldness to do even greater things.

God has placed you in a God-fearing family who will support you as you choose His way. You are not alone. He has created you for greatness. Grab hold of God and move into your destiny. You will soon find yourselves in places you could never have dreamed of and reaching heights you never would have imagined. By God's grace, you'll accomplish much when you extend your faith and rise above the giants in your mind. Remember, situations are rarely as big or as bad as you may have imagined. You have victory over fear in Jesus' name.

All my love,
Nana

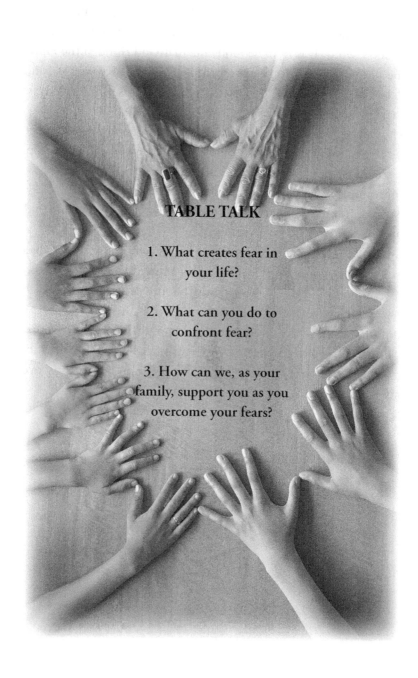

TABLE TALK

1. What creates fear in your life?

2. What can you do to confront fear?

3. How can we, as your family, support you as you overcome your fears?

9

Life Will Have its Difficulties

Life's difficulties and roadblocks can strengthen your faith

That is why, for Christ's sake, I delight in weaknesses, in insults, in hardships, in persecutions, in difficulties. For when I am weak, then I am strong.
—2 Corinthians 12:10

A positive perspective will empower us to navigate whatever comes our way. My dad exemplified a stand-up posture in dealing with blindness. Papa, athletic and fit most of his life, dealt heroically with the unfortunate hand he received. In his early forties, he lost the ability to drive and was considered disabled by his early fifties. Papa courageously chose to move forward in new ways. When he was no longer able to work his factory job, he worked inside the home, helping with the cooking, cleaning, and upkeep. Papa took pride in being there for his wife, children, and grandchildren. His poor sight didn't stop him from traveling by bus to Connecticut to help me with my daughters after I had minor surgery. It didn't even stop him from establishing his own small lawn care business. Not once did I ever hear him whine or feel sorry for himself. He gathered the lemons life gave him and made lemonade. It was through his loss of sight I gained a clearer vision of what really matters in life. One of Papa's favorite dishes to both cook and eat was a Cape Verdean rice and beans staple called Jagacida (aka Jag).

Here's to you, Papa! Thank you!

Recipe #9: Jagacida (Cape Verdean Rice and Beans) (pg. 144)

My Dear Grandchildren,

One of Nana's most salient traits is to face reality in the midst of life's difficult situations. Like most grandmothers, my desire would be to protect and save you from all hardships, but unfortunately, that is impossible. What I can and will do is "pray you through" these challenges. The reality is life can be painfully difficult at times. But my dear grandchildren, never despair—have hope. In the midst of our trials, we have our faith in God to lean upon for support.

Through life's difficult experiences, God has always shown Himself faithful. Placing my trust in Him and choosing His ways has always led me to safety. However, let me warn you. When faced with struggles, we become more spiritually vulnerable. This is often the time Satan will try to sow fear and doubt into our mind and spirit. Be aware of his attempts to bring discouragement and know that you can take authority over him. You are never alone. God says, "I will never leave you nor forsake you." (Deuteronomy 31:8) He will always be there to guide you to victory.

Keep in mind this truth; nothing takes God by surprise. He never promised our journey would be trouble-free. In fact, Jesus said quite the opposite in John 16:33. "I have told you these things, so that in me you may have peace. In this world you will have trouble. But take heart, I have overcome the world."

Trouble will come and trouble will go, but God is always there and will use the experience to strengthen you. We are created for God's glory. He knows what we must go through to prepare and perfect us for the work He has assigned for us.

One of Nana's most difficult experiences as a teenager happened in her first year of college. I went from being the most popular girl in high school to one of the most unpopular girls in my all-women's college. It was in the 1970s and Nana's college was in Boston, Massachusetts. At that time, Boston was quite racially divided. In fact, the high school next door to my college was being forced to integrate and became the focal point of racial strife. Every day there were armed National Guard soldiers outside the school as our African American youth entered in the morning and departed in the afternoon. The guards were there to protect the students as well as keep peace inside and outside the school.

In previous decades, this sort of thing happened in the Deep South, but it was my first time experiencing this in the North. Tensions were high, and if you were of color, you needed to be careful wherever you traveled in the city.

Nana had the experience of being brought up in a small city neighborhood of color until she was eight years old. At the age of nine, my parents built a house in the suburbs where everyone was Caucasian. To make myself comfortable in all environments, I chose to look at people's character rather than at the color of their skin.

In college, my friends were from both races. Because of this choice, some of my African American sisters chose to alienate me. They would often talk negatively about me and intentionally exclude me from their gatherings.

As a college student, it was challenging enough adjusting to living away from home, never mind having other people trying to make life more difficult. It was a very lonely time but rather than feeling sorry for myself, God became my constant companion. It was my choice to go to college to get a good education. Academics became my primary focus.

Most days I was at the library until early evening. What Satan meant for evil, God meant for good because Nana ended up graduating cum laude (with honors). Ironically, the girls who caused me grief were the same girls, who in my junior year asked me to tutor them. I was happy to do so. I learned to extend forgiveness to others through this challenging time. God taught me many lessons in that painful period, using it to strengthen and mold me.

Looking back over my life, God clearly used my college years as preparation for full-time ministry. In ministry, it is often necessary to stand alone and stay focused on doing the right thing, no matter what.

My dear grandchildren, learn to look to God in your times of trouble. He will never leave you nor forsake you. The difficulties will mold you, not break you. Remember, Nana will be praying for you.

All my love,
Nana

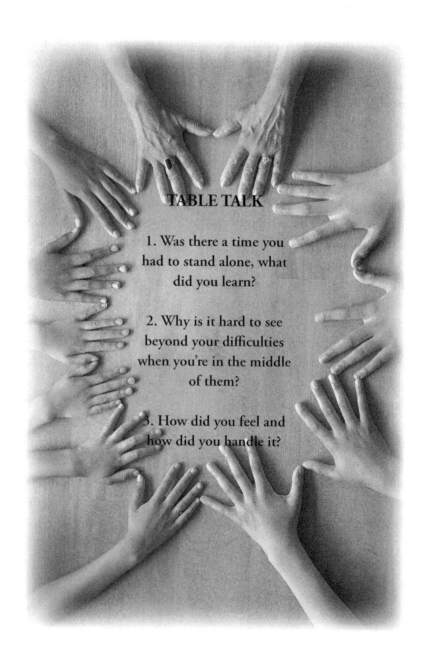

TABLE TALK

1. Was there a time you had to stand alone, what did you learn?

2. Why is it hard to see beyond your difficulties when you're in the middle of them?

3. How did you feel and how did you handle it?

10

Enjoy the Journey

Being observant on your journey will provide many
God-given life lessons

*Rejoice always, pray continually, give thanks in all circumstances; for this is
God's will for you in Christ Jesus. —1 Thessalonians 5:16-18*

It was a blessing to grow up next door to my paternal grandparents. My grandfather was a longshoreman who had access to seafood fresh off the fishing boat. Every few weeks on a Friday afternoon, Nana Lopes would tape a note to our back door that read, "Dinner is at our house tonight. Don't cook, just come on over." I loved those Fridays when the extended family gathered spontaneously at my grandparents' house for a seafood feast.

My favorite meal was Nana's homemade clam chowder. No one made chowder better than Nana. But more than the food, I loved the way the family left jobs, responsibilities, and worries behind and simply enjoyed one another. Those special Fridays around Nana and Grandpa's table were filled with great food, good conversation, and plenty of laughter.

Acknowledge and embrace such precious memories. They will uplift your spirits throughout the course of your life's journey.

Recipe #10: Nana Lopes' Creamy Clam Chowder (pg. 144)

My Dear Grandchildren,

Sometimes being too focused on getting to our destiny causes us to completely miss what God is doing along the way. Be determined to pay close attention to what God is revealing in any given moment. He frequently molds, teaches, and shows us great and mighty things as we simply go about our days.

For my 58th birthday, the Lord created a wonderful opportunity to spend time with my family taking a hike up Sleeping Giant Mountain. Grandad and I had often hiked the mountain with our two young daughters, Erica and Stefanie. It was always something we enjoyed doing as a family. This would be our first hike with our grandchildren; Luke who was five and Chase who was four.

In my opinion, life does not get any better than being surrounded by loved ones. The thought of being able to climb Sleeping Giant with my grandsons, my daughter, son-in-law, and husband made it extra special. God provided the most perfect weather—the sun was shining, the temperature was in the low eighties, and the wind was only slightly blowing.

We started with excitement and great zeal, determined to reach our destination—the tower at the top of the mountain. Not too far into the hike, four-year-old Chase began to whine asking if we were almost there. The tower was over a mile up the winding trail. I knew our hike was going to feel a lot longer than we had anticipated, especially to the legs of our young children.

Auntie Erica kept the spirit upbeat by sharing stories of her childhood Sleeping Giant hiking experiences. Her sense of adventure and enthusiasm helped for a while, at least until the sighting of the first dogs along the trail. Luke and Chase are not dog lovers and were not ashamed to vocalize it. With some reassurance from their dad and grandad, they navigated the threat and continued the journey.

As we proceeded, Chase began to complain he was tired and asked his father to carry him on his shoulders. Uncle Dwain obliged and carried him uphill quite a distance—not a small feat. Luke, who was only five at the time, did well, sometimes needing a little handholding, but overall remained a trooper. The trail turned out to be a lot longer than I remembered. "The tower is just around the bend" was my confident and repeated declaration.

Hearing myself say it over and over only to be proven wrong caused me to readjust my focus.

I made a conscious decision to take my mind, and everyone else's, off the destination and simply enjoy the journey. Yes, the journey certainly had its challenges, but the memories we were creating were far more precious than the view from the top. Just being together with family and experiencing this challenge brought so much joy.

A mile and a half from our starting point, we finally reached the lookout tower at the top of the mountain. It took a lot of encouragement from the adults, some handholding, some piggyback rides, but we did it. . . and we are still enjoying those memories. We reached our destiny because we were there for one another. It was a wonderful family outing, filled with lots of sunshine and the joy of simple life lessons learned together with the people we love.

In life there will be God-given goals and desires you want to accomplish, but your greatest lessons will unfold while working to achieve them. Always be mindful and observant about what God is doing and showing you while still in route.

Look around. Who can use your help along the way? Who might need a word of encouragement? Who would benefit from a shoulder to lean on? Always be cognizant of the people who surround you. You have been placed near them for a purpose; God may very well desire to use you in their lives. He has a plan and purpose for you to fulfill every day. At times, all we need to do is take a step back to recognize God's hand. Remember, my dear grandchildren, the journey is just as important as the destination.

All my love,
Nana

TABLE TALK

1. What does it mean to just "enjoy the journey"?

2. Has God ever spoken to you through a situation or circumstance?

3. What was His message?

11

A Man of Faith

A portrait of a godly, contemporary man of faith who walks
in righteousness and sacrifice

*But you, man of God, flee from all this, and pursue righteousness, godliness,
faith, love, endurance and gentleness. Fight the good fight of the faith. Take hold
of the eternal life to which you were called when you made your good confession
in the presence of many witnesses. —1 Timothy 6:11-12*

In 1975, on a cold February evening in Boston, I met the man who would
become my husband. He was a blind date my brother and cousin arranged
without my knowledge. I would not have gone if I had known what they were
doing. When I met him, they introduced him as Chris. I called him Chris all
evening. I didn't know his real name until the next day when he called me on
the phone and shared that his close friends and family called him Todd. That
really made me very suspicious. All I could think was he had an "alias" and
perhaps he was trying to hide something. When questioned, he explained
when he came to college in Boston, he thought the name Todd was not cool
enough, so he took the name "Chris" from Christian, his middle name, and
told everyone his name was Chris. There are still about three college friends
that call him Chris. I'm glad my dear husband, your grandfather, eventually
came to accept his given name, and went on to have an even greater name—
servant of God. One of my husband's favorite entrees is lasagna.

Recipe #11: Nannie's Lasagna (pg. 145)

My Dear Grandchildren,

The apostle Paul in the book of Timothy encourages his spiritual son to pursue righteousness, godliness, faith, love, endurance, and gentleness. When pondering these traits, there is one man that comes to mind and that is your honorable grandfather, "Grandad" Todd Foster.

I met your grandad when we were nineteen-year-old teenagers. Back then, he sported a curly lopsided Afro hairstyle. I thought he was rather cute but had some reservations knowing he wasn't a Christian. Over time, we became good friends. About six months into our friendship, Grandad received Christ as his savior. From that point on, my heart recognized him as the man for me. When Grandad gave his heart to the Lord, he began to read his Bible and submit and surrender different areas of his life to God. Like all of us, he was not perfect, but Grandad continued to let God do a good work in him.

Little did we know all the Lord had in store for us. The two of us never thought in our wildest dreams we would end up in full-time ministry, although Grandad was always faithful in serving the Lord. He started as an usher, then progressed to a Sunday School teacher, and before we knew it God was "calling" him into full-time ministry as an Associate Pastor. Two years later, he was appointed Senior Pastor of our church.

Grandad took a real leap of faith to answer the call on his life. He held a great job with the local phone company and was being trained for a high-level management position when God called him. Grandad stepped down from his secular job to answer the call to ministry for half the salary. It was not a decision either of us took lightly, as by that time we had a hefty mortgage and two little girls to ultimately put through college.

Todd C. Foster

I am so proud of the "man of God" Grandad has become and have watched him over the years make some very difficult decisions. In his decision-making he has always chosen to do things God's way, with righteousness and sacrifice. Grandad could have used his position as Senior Pastor as an opportunity to meet his own needs, but he never did. In fact, he has done just the opposite—always trying to uplift others and bring life to those around him. There have been times Grandad ended up with the short end of the stick, but he has never complained—he just continued to pray and trust God.

Your grandfather, my husband, is an honorable man who like Timothy walks in righteousness, godliness, faith, love, endurance, and gentleness. People have walked away from Grandad when they did not get their way, but he continued to stand on godly principles and pray for them. When the same people needed a helping hand, who but Grandad was there to help them. His compassion and spirit of love exemplify how a Christian should conduct themselves in all situations.

We are blessed to have Grandad as the patriarch of our family. His faith has been both a light and an example for all of us to follow. I am so proud to be his wife and you should be very proud to be his grandchildren, his legacy. Grandad, Pastor Todd C. Foster, we love and respect you. Continue to lead the way. We are following you as you follow Christ.

All my love,
Nana

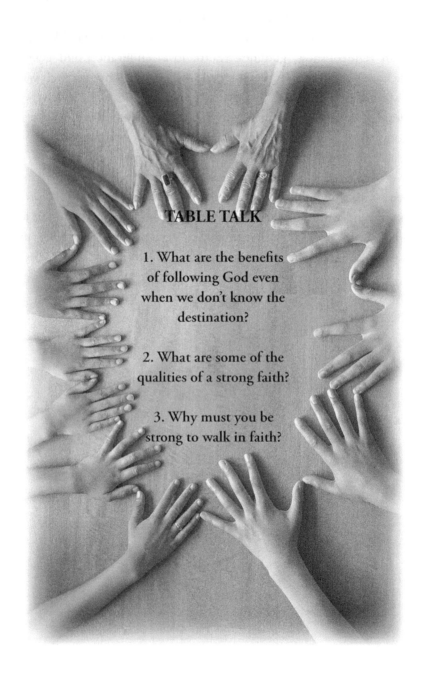

TABLE TALK

1. What are the benefits of following God even when we don't know the destination?

2. What are some of the qualities of a strong faith?

3. Why must you be strong to walk in faith?

12

Depend on the Holy Spirit

The Holy Spirit is an on-time helper who will teach,
comfort, and guide

When you are brought before synagogues, rulers and authorities, do not worry about how you will defend yourselves or what you will say, for the Holy Spirit will teach you at that time what you should say. —Luke 12:11-12

When my youngest was about six years old, she and my mother-in-law stopped at a local convenience store for a quart of milk. As they were exiting the store, my daughter had an ominous sense that something bad was about to happen. "Grandma," she said, "let's go! I feel like something bad is about to happen."

When they got into the car and began to pull away, there was a sudden, large explosion in the gas station directly next door to the convenience store. The Holy Spirit gave my daughter a warning. His is a voice we do well to heed.

Here's to a quart of milk, a still small voice, and a gracious God who has much to share with us. My mother-in-law was famous for her homemade eggnog. As you turn milk into nog, consider what the Holy Spirit might very well be trying to say in order to guide, protect, and edify you.

Recipe #12: Eggnog a la Jean (pg. 145)

My Dear Grandchildren,

In your lives, there will be times when the words you speak will greatly influence your destiny. It will be imperative your words bring forth life. The Bible tells us there is power in the words we speak. "The tongue has the power of life and death, and those who love it will eat its fruit." (Proverbs 18:21)

In this Christian walk, it is crucial to be "prayed-up" on a daily basis. Being prayed up means you have sought the Lord and asked Him to accomplish His will in your life for that day. Always remember, as a Christian, you have been given a helper who will teach, counsel, and guide you. He is the Holy Spirit, the third person of the Trinity. The Holy Spirit is given to all who receive Christ as their savior. It is our responsibility to develop a close relationship with Him. The closer the relationship we have with Him, the more we will hear God's voice inside of us. I've heard Christians say, "Something told me not to do that or to go a certain way." That SOMETHING is actually someone, the Holy Spirit. Always pray and learn to listen to God's voice. It's a voice that will keep you on the right path, guide you in the direction you should go, and at the precise moment, give you the right words to speak.

God has great plans for you, my grandchildren. At times you will be put before people who will have the authority to invite you into specific chapters of your God-given destiny. They will decide whether you will get into the particular school you've applied to, get that great job you are qualified for, or win the spot you want on a sports team. When you are put before influential people, do not worry about what you are to say, but ask the Lord for the very words to speak.

Luke 12:11-12 reminds us not to worry about how you are to defend yourself or what you will say, for the Holy Spirit will teach you at that precise moment. Like all people, you will be placed in situations when you'll be searching for a good answer. Don't let that concern you—you have the Holy Spirit, whom if asked, will guide you. Then, after you have spoken, trust God for the outcome. Ultimately, God has the final say regarding our destiny and we want our words to be in alignment with, and not a hindrance to His will.

There have been many times in Nana's life where she just didn't have the words to speak. But when I leaned on the Holy Spirit and asked for assistance, God was faithful. One incident never to be forgotten was when I was interviewing for my first teaching position. My eldest daughter was in kindergarten at Westhills Magnet School in New Haven. Her principal, a woman by the name of Ms. Tiani, called and said she had gotten my name from the Board of Ed., and wanted to interview me. Having watched Ms. Tiani, she seemed so tough on her teachers I was somewhat intimidated by her. I was inwardly thinking I'd be open to teaching at any school in New Haven, anywhere that is, except Westhills.

When Ms. Tiani called, my heart was beating hard. She asked me to come in for an interview and my high regard for the school led me to agree. In the interview Ms. Tiani said, "So tell me why you want to teach here." My heart skipped a beat and I began to inwardly call upon God to give me the words to speak. The Holy Spirit was saying, "Speak the truth."

With a deep breath, my response was, "Ms. Tiani, quite honestly, I don't want to teach here because I've watched you with your teachers and you can be very intimidating." There was nothing to lose by speaking the truth because it was not my desire to work there anyway. Ms. Tiani laughed and then stood up and excused herself from the room. Two minutes later she returned and said to me, "I called downtown and told them to take your name off the "placement" list—you have the job."

While sitting in that office totally stunned by what had just happened, it nevertheless seemed to me God had spoken in the matter. I had peace about accepting the challenge and took the job. My first teaching assignment was difficult, but boy, did it strengthen and shape me into a strong teacher. Having received great training at Westhills, I rejoice to this day the Holy Spirit gave me the right words to speak, and God's plan was fulfilled.

My dear grandchildren, when you find yourself in a place where you do not know what to do or what to say—lean into the Holy Spirit and get His counsel. You will never be misguided. You will never regret taking His counsel. The Holy Spirit will bring you nothing less than an abundant life. Love you to the moon and back!

All my love,
Nana

TABLE TALK

1. If the Holy Spirit has ever spoken to you, what did He say? Did you obey?

2. Why do you think God gave us the Holy Spirit?

3. Can you tell the difference between the Holy Spirit and your own spirit's voice?

13

Faithfulness

Be faithful to walk God's path while developing the gifts
and talents He has given you

I have chosen the way of faithfulness; I have set my heart on your laws.
—Psalm 119:30

As a child I had the opportunity to accompany my paternal grandparents to the bogs of Cape Cod to pick cranberries. For my grandparents, it was a tedious backbreaking job that was done on their knees with the aid of a handheld cranberry scoop. It was done in autumn and provided extra income for the winter months. As they picked cranberries, I enjoyed running up and down the sand dunes. Their lives were filled with hard, manual labor, so different than the life I have been able to experience.

God has a unique recipe for each of our lives. It requires the exact ingredients of opportunities and experiences along with the precise order in which they must be put together. Some of the ingredients will be things we like, and others, well, not so much.

Just like a Master Chef, God is good at turning our lives into something best suited to serve His purposes. Trust the Creator and resist the temptation to take shortcuts or do it your own way. He knows exactly what He's doing. We need to seek His plan for our lives and be faithful to follow it to the letter. The outcome will be glorious!

The recipe for Cranberry Good'n Pudding in the appendix has all the ingredients and steps for you to make something my family absolutely loves. Feel free to alter it to your taste but leave God's recipe for your life alone.

Recipe #13: Cranberry Good'n Puddin (pg. 146)

My Dear Grandchildren,

Throughout life you will be presented with opportunities that have the potential to carry you in many different directions. God will call you to walk one path, but the world will try to lure you in an entirely different way. Although it can be wonderful to have choices, it is paramount to discern God's ordained course for your life. You'll always find the God-ordained choices to be the most fruitful; He will receive glory and you will be blessed. Faithfulness requires us to walk the path God desires and operate in the gifts and talents He has bestowed upon us. You'll need to learn to use your God-given gifts and talents in everyday life and so become precisely who He has created you to be.

Look at yourself and take inventory of how you have been equipped by the Lord. What makes you unique? What should you develop to bring glory to God? Is it your wonderful singing voice, athletic talent, humorous personality, your way with fashion, or your kindness to all? What makes you wonderfully and uniquely YOU? Whatever your uniqueness is, you will need to be faithful to develop it to the glory of God. God is watching to see how you utilize what He has given you. Be faithful with what you have been given. Do not take it for granted. The Bible says, "If we will be faithful in the small things" God will increase and entrust us with more. (Luke 16:10). Remember, only God can open the doors leading to an abundant life.

What does faithfulness look like? From my experience, faithfulness begins by seeking God in prayer. We first must seek God to discern His will regarding what we are to pursue. When you are sure God is leading you in a certain direction, you must be determined to follow. As soon as you decide to follow God's path, you will begin to hear the voice of Satan question or challenge your decision. Satan will begin to ask, "Are you sure you want to do that?" "Is that what God said?" "It's going to be difficult." "You don't have the money to accomplish that." He will go on and on to discourage you.

Hear me, my dear grandchildren, ignore Satan's taunting. Get God's final word on the matter and then begin to move in that direction with all that is within you. God opens doors when we place our trust in Him and take steps of faith to move in obedience to His directives. Place one foot in front of the other and walk it out. You will be amazed at the opportunities presented to you. Yes, there will be obstacles and difficult times, but God will see you through as you walk in obedience to whatever He has called you to pursue.

Being faithful to God is not always easy. It will sometimes put you at odds with those you love and may cause you to feel like you're walking alone. Do not get discouraged for you are never alone—God promises, "He will never leave us nor forsake us" (Deuteronomy 31:6). He will be with you through the completion of whatever He has called you to do. There will be satisfaction in your spirit when you see yourself accomplishing God's will. You will look back at the obstacles you have overcome and realize they have contributed to making you a stronger person.

Seek the Lord every day and obtain your strength from His word. Work hard to obediently pursue everything God has called you to achieve. If you do your part, God will do His. Faithfulness is maintained with endurance and perseverance. Both are birthed out of an intentional decision to stay the course no matter what. Every God-directed task we complete will produce a harvest. Be faithful to the task or direction God has given you and you will experience "the goodness of the Lord in the land of the living." (Psalm 27:13). You will be blessed on this side of eternity if you choose the way of faithfulness.

All my love,
Nana

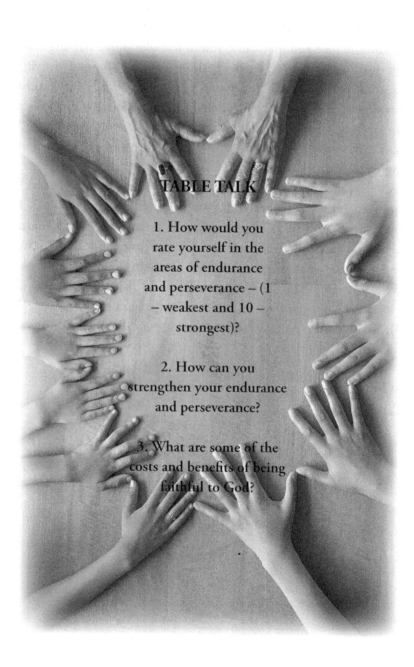

TABLE TALK

1. How would you rate yourself in the areas of endurance and perseverance – (1 – weakest and 10 – strongest)?

2. How can you strengthen your endurance and perseverance?

3. What are some of the costs and benefits of being faithful to God?

PRACTICAL LIFE LESSONS

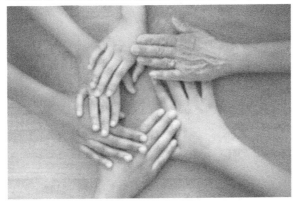

14

Be Your Authentic Self

You are uniquely fashioned and destined with purpose to
fulfill God's earthly plan

*For by the grace given me I say to every one of you: Do not think of yourself
more highly than you ought, but rather think of yourself with sober judgment, in
accordance with the faith God has distributed to each of you. —Romans 12:3*

A friend of ours invited us over for his homemade lobster bisque. It was
quite tasty, and the company and conversation were even better. We
found out after the meal that the bisque was prepared with langostino and
not real lobster. Langostino is a reasonable substitute in a recipe for good old
Maine lobster and it goes for about half the price. It's from the same family,
but it's not the same.

When it comes to enjoying lobster all by itself, I prefer the real thing.
As the old song used to say, "Ain't nothing like the real thing, baby!" Boil it
whole, or bake the tail, add butter, surround yourself with friends and family,
and you've got more than a meal. You've got all the makings of a memorable
event. Just make sure the people you invite over are as real as the lobster.
Enjoy our recipe for baked lobster tail.

Recipe #14: Baked Lobster Tail (pg. 147)

My Dear Grandchildren,

We live in a time where people often exaggerate the circumstances in their lives to impress others. With the popularity of social media and "reality" shows, it seems many people are posturing to appear as celebrities. It saddens me to think people are so insecure in who they are they feel the need to appear to be something they are not. There is no need to be deceptive or dishonest. All you ever need to be in life is your genuine self.

As Christians, we are to live and present ourselves authentically. We do ourselves, and the world, a disservice when we are not genuine. In Christ, the person God created is enough. There is no one exactly like you; nor anyone who can fulfill the plans and purposes God has uniquely ordained for you. The very best one can ever be is the fully developed "you" God has designed. God created us and loves us just the way we are but desires our growth in the knowledge of Him. As we grow by the inner work of the Holy Spirit, we will become more like Him.

My dear grandchild, for God's sake and your own peace and joy, resist the temptation to make yourself out to be something you are not. You are a child of God. In Romans 12:3 it says, "Do not think of yourself more highly than you ought, but rather think of yourself with sober judgment, in accordance with the faith God has distributed to each of you." In other words, be humble and genuine by keeping God central in your identity. Grow in His grace and allow the increasing brightness of His life to shine through you.

Jesus was the Son of God but walked this earth as a humble servant. We too are to walk with humble authenticity. To walk in authenticity, you will need to take time to learn who you are in Christ. Once you've learned who you are in Christ, you will appreciate and utilize the gifts God has placed within you. Realize all we are and all we have is because of God. The gifts we have been given by God are to be given away for the benefit of others.

If we could view each other through God's eyes, we'd see the great value He has placed in each of us. In the natural realm, we often look at one another and long for the qualities and

Joseph W. Christian

attributes others possess. It is fine to admire the good qualities we see in others and even be inspired to work on ourselves to develop such qualities in our own lives. We should always be appreciative of who God has created us to be and develop ourselves to bring glory to His name. Let's celebrate each other and find ways in which we can complement one another.

One of the most genuine, humble accomplished men in our family was Grandad's maternal grandfather, Joseph Warfield Christian (he was Gigi's father). Grandad Christian was brought up in an age when African Americans were extremely oppressed and discriminated against. To Grandad's credit, he went to a two-year college and was highly successful in the business world. In fact, he was one of the first African Americans to own a marketing firm in New York City. His firm had Joseph E. Seagram as one of his corporate clients. He knew several well-known entertainers, athletes, and businesspeople such as jazz singer Ella Fitzgerald, and professional baseball players Monte Irvin and Willie Mays, to name a few. He also had scores of trophies for his bowling, billiards, and golf skills. With all Grandad Christian's accomplishments, we never heard him brag or embellish. Because of his humility, God was able to lead him to success. Although Grandad Christian achieved a degree of financial security, he chose to live a life of simplicity. He was a dignified, quiet man who left a legacy for his family in a time when the odds were stacked against him.

Remember my grandchildren, there is no need to "posture" yourself, for you are worthy in Christ. Embark on a journey with Christ to find out who He made you to be. Others may look up to you for guidance. Be genuine and give of yourself. You are the recipient of a strong family legacy—you must endeavor to pay it forward. To whom much is given, much will be expected.

All my love,
Nana

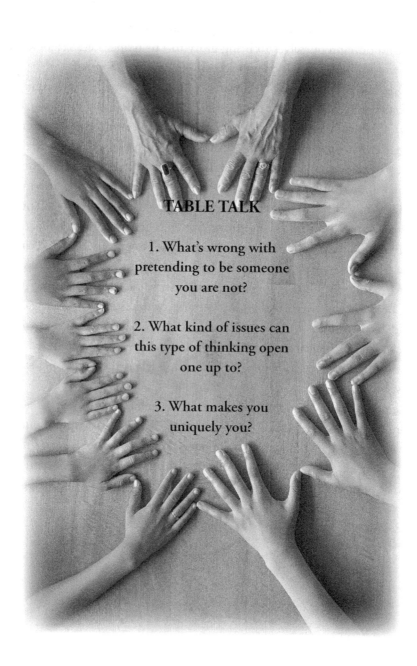

TABLE TALK

1. What's wrong with pretending to be someone you are not?

2. What kind of issues can this type of thinking open one up to?

3. What makes you uniquely you?

15

Noble Woman

A wise woman navigates the seasons in her life by creating a
legacy of love

*A wife of noble character who can find? She is worth far more than rubies. Her
husband has full confidence in her and lacks nothing of value. She is clothed
with strength and dignity; she can laugh at the days to come. She speaks with
wisdom, and faithful instruction is on her tongue. She watches over the affairs of
her household and does not eat the bread of idleness. Her children arise and call
her blessed; her husband also, and he praises her: Many women do noble things,
but you surpass them all. —Proverbs 31:10-11, 25-29*

As time has progressed, women have made substantial advancement in
being able to sit at the decision-making tables in our nation. My belief is
that women can have it "all" but not "all" at the same time. We have seasons
in our lives. Those who have young children should keep their family as their
main priority. As children grow into teenagers and young adults, priorities can
begin to shift toward the dreams and desires God has placed within us. The
"crown" of a well-lived prioritized life will be a thriving family whose children
serve the Lord, walk in their purposes, and continue the family legacy.

A woman "whose recipe for life" includes pouring herself into family will
enjoy an honorable legacy. My husband's grandmother was a woman who
kept her family as her priority. She lived on a riverbank where blue claw crabs
were readily available, and often served fresh crab cakes. Her fresh crab cakes
were made after hours of lovingly shucking crabs by hand.

Recipe #15: Delmarva Crab Cakes (pg. 148)

My Dear Grandchildren,

We live in a day where women continue to fight for equal rights as well as for their place in society. This struggle for gender equality has at times required women to fight to gain what should rightfully and legally be theirs. Despite the progress that's been made, there are still some gender divides when it comes to opportunities for women. We are oftentimes asked to choose between our families or our careers—a decision most men will never have to face. Our struggle to progress has been exhausting and has even caused us to question our role and value in society. The verses in Proverbs 31 refreshingly portray a woman who walked triumphantly in the virtues of love, honor, and respect as she went busily about her days.

A woman who possessed these three virtues was Nana Christian, Grandad Foster's maternal grandmother. Myrtle (Sterrett) Christian was a diminutive, quiet, and loving woman who possessed both inner and outer beauty. Although Nana Christian never spoke much about her relationship with God, it was evident by the way she lived her life that she both loved and respected Him.

Nana Christian was born and raised in the state of Delaware, and she long carried a passion for her beloved state. Although married life took her to New York City, she forever remained a country girl at heart. Prior to retirement, Nana and Grandad Christian purchased a modest home perched on a hill overlooking the Indian River in Millsboro, Delaware. Given the slow pace and serenity of the rural community, they moved there permanently upon Grandad Christian's retirement. Grandad Foster and his brother Uncle Ron spent many of their summers visiting their grandparents on the Indian River.

Myrtle S. Christian

Nana Christian's Delaware home was always warm and invitingly filled with the sweet aromas of homemade biscuits, scrapple, crab cakes, blueberry pie, and peach cobbler, to name a few. A visit to Delaware was a culinary treat to say the least. Her home was always filled with love, peace, and home-cooked meals. Although she was always warm and loving, she best demonstrated her love through her hospitality and skills in the kitchen—rising early in the morning to start her food preparation for the day. Taking care of her family brought her much joy.

Nana Christian once shared with me what it was like living through the Great Depression of the 1920s-30s. It was the one time in her life she worked at a job outside of the home due to the wartime labor shortage of men. She explained to me that the Depression taught her to be frugal with money and to always maintain a good amount of savings to ensure that her family would have an emergency fund in times of need. From the sidelines, Nana Christian adored and supported her husband in all his endeavors. Her shyness and dislike of the limelight made her feel more comfortable there.

Nana Christian operated in a very traditional woman's role and was very content to do so. Her priority was always her family and their welfare. Because of this, to be in her presence was to feel loved and valued. Her steadfast love and devotion to her family left us a beautiful legacy that has been passed down from one generation to the next. There is something to be said about a person who loves and empowers others. Don't get me wrong, Nana Christian did pursue her own hobbies and interests. In addition to being an excellent cook, she excelled in crafting, knitting, sewing, and much more. She was also an exemplary housekeeper, keeping an immaculately organized home. As a young married woman, a great deal was gleaned from her on my Delaware visits. Nana Christian never did anything halfway. Everything she put her hands to she did in a spirit of excellence.

The Proverbs 31 woman will forever bring Nana Christian to my remembrance. Grandad Christian could certainly say:

"She was clothed with strength and dignity; she can laugh at the days to come. She speaks with wisdom, and faithful instruction is on her tongue. She watches over the affairs of her household and does not eat the bread of idleness. Her children arise and call her blessed; her husband also, and he praises her: 'Many women do noble things, but you surpass them all.'"

My dear granddaughters, although times have changed and women have many more opportunities and choices than Nana Christian, let us always put our families first and let them know they are esteemed and loved. Always remember as you embark on your journey, there are "seasons" in a woman's life. Know your gifts and talents will create opportunities, but always ask yourself, "Is this the right season?" You will never regret having chosen to give love and devotion to your family in its season. God will bring forth the right opportunities in the right season of your life. You won't miss out on anything God has for you. Your season of life will help to guide you in your decisions. Choose wisely in each season. Like Nana Christian, you will create a legacy of love. Your love will flow from generation to generation and you, too, will be crowned a Proverbs 31 woman. Thank you, Nana Christian. Your love continues to flow through us all.

All my love,
Nana

TABLE TALK

1. What season of your life
are you in today?

2. What is your focus for
this season?

3. What can you do to
create and strengthen
your legacy of love in your
family?

16

That You Would be Courageous

May you possess the ability to stand alone with God in the
midst of adversity

Be on your guard; stand firm in the faith; be courageous; be strong.
—1 Corinthians16:13

Many of my own relatives, and the relatives of my sons-in-law, immigrated to America for a better life. The unknowns were many, yet they exercised courage in their decision to leave behind their home country and move forward into uncharted territory. Their courage has opened a new world of opportunity for many of us. We stand upon their shoulders and embrace the new prospects presented. Never forget, our ancestors' courage created the opportunities for the abundant life we now experience. An unwavering trust in God undoubtedly was the main ingredient in their acts of courage.

We're all Americans now, yet proud of our heritage. Apple pie is as American as recipes get. You can find the recipe for Nana Christian's Apple Pie in the appendix.

Recipe #16: Nana Christian's Apple Pie (pg. 149)

My Dear Grandchildren,

When pondering what you will need to be a fruitful Christian, the word "courageous" comes to mind. The world we live in has deteriorated greatly on my generation's watch. What the world has turned upside down, to the extent that it's within your power to do so, you must accept the challenge to courageously correct.

Jesus Christ is the same yesterday, today, and forever. (Hebrews 13:8) Christ never changes, nor do His principles. The mindset and morality of this world may have changed, but God's Word remains the same. My prayer for you, my grandchildren, is for God to enable you to be courageous young men and women. May you be shining lights who personify God's principles and character in a darkened sinful world. It is my desire for you, but I realize it will not be easy to accomplish.

To be courageous means you will need to be brave, bold, strong, and yet loving. You will need to remove yourself from those who are asking you to go the wrong way and do the wrong thing. It also means you will need wisdom to make the right decisions and learn to stand by yourself in the face of adversity. At times, you will be required to speak up for the less fortunate and those on the outskirts of society, even in the face of being ridiculed. During these times, please remember that "God will never leave you nor forsake you" (Deuteronomy 31:6)—you will never be alone. To be courageous, you will have to know who you are in Christ Jesus and trust that His word is true.

Always remember, my dear ones, you were created for God's glory. You were not created just to fill space here on this earth. You are to be examples of righteousness that are tempered with an overflowing love for God and your fellow brothers and sisters. ("Dear friends, since God so loved us, we also ought to love one another." 1 John 4:11)

The word "courageous" brings to mind a wonderful story relayed to me about Luke, my eldest grandson. His fourth-grade teacher pulled my daughter aside to say how his actions touched her heart. The teacher shared how during recess the boys were forming teams to play football. There was one little boy with developmental challenges who the other boys wanted to keep out of the game for fear that he would hurt their chances of winning. But Luke stood up for the boy and simply declared to the others, "He's playing!" End of story.

No discussion. No debate. The other boys quickly changed their minds and let the little boy play.

That day, Luke displayed what it means to be courageous. His thinking could have been, "Well, I'll just go along with everyone else and not make any waves," but no, he did what he knew was the right thing to do. Because of Luke's courage, a little boy felt embraced and loved with the love of God and a classroom of boys saw God in action because of Luke's righteousness and strength.

Luke was only 10 years old when this happened, but he made the "God Difference" in the lives of many. This story of courage touches my heart so very much and reassures me that Grandad and I will have a fruitful legacy.

As you live your lives, my dear grandchildren, be strong, be steadfast in the Word of God you have been taught. Be courageous, to live out and walk in the Word. It never changes and continues to bring forth life and remains true. Shine, grandchildren, shine—be courageous!

All my love,
Nana

TABLE TALK

1. When have you chosen to be courageous and why?

2. What were the results of your courageous action?

3. Who is one of the most courageous people you know and what makes them courageous?

17

Money: Its Importance and Its Place

The practical benefits of wisely handling and managing
God's money

*For the love of money is the root of all kinds of evil. Some people, eager for
money, have wandered from the faith and pierced themselves with many
griefs.—1 Timothy 6:10*

One of my sweetest childhood memories is of my great-grandfather,
cane-in-hand, walking uptown on Purchase Street in New Bedford,
Massachusetts to pay his bills. He had seven children, several grandchildren,
and even more great-grandchildren. Sometimes as he passed by our elementary
school, we would be outside for recess. When seeing him, a sense of pride
would well up in me because he was always impeccably dressed in a suit
and tie complemented by a stiff, starched white shirt. No less than five or
six great-grandchildren would run up to greet and hug him. He'd warmly
embrace us and give each of us some money. My great-grandfather was by
no means rich but giving money to his great-grandchildren was his way of
saying, "I love you." There is no one recipe for showing our love. Love can
be demonstrated in so many ways. One dessert recipe often made and given
away to express love in our family is Magic Cookie Bars.

Recipe #17: Magic Cookie Bars (pg. 150)

My Dear Grandchildren,

It is so very important to be knowledgeable about the handling and management of money. As a young adult, handling money was one area where I felt inadequate. As a newlywed, I remember asking my parents why they never taught us about managing and investing money. Their answer was "because we didn't have money." Their response surprised me, because growing up we lacked for nothing. From my perspective, we seemed to have everything we needed and then some.

Thinking back about my parents and my upbringing, there were certainly some very practical financial lessons acquired through observing their day-to-day living. Some lessons learned were "Always live within or beneath your means." "A charge card is not your friend." "Never charge more than what you can pay off in that month."

As a little girl, my recollection was that my mom liked quality things, items just a little more than we could afford. She'd often admire these things and then begin to save her money to buy them. She was always very conscious of the family budget and very careful to stay within the boundaries of that budget.

As a way for Nannie and Papa to keep within their family budget, they owned only one car. That one car had to drop everyone off at work and school. Having one car forced us to be together all the time and helped knit us into a close family.

Another thing my parents did was to budget on a weekly basis. Every week, they would cash their paychecks and place money into paper envelopes labeled with the names of bills that needed to be paid. At the end of the month, there would be enough in those envelopes to pay all the bills. That budget always included a "savings" envelope to hold the "just in case money" for any unexpected needs. Anything left over after the budget envelopes were filled might mean a special trip to Roger's Dairy for ice cream or Gene's Fish and Chips for fried clams—a real treat indeed.

Nannie and Papa Lopes were also very big on "earned" allowances. Uncle Carl and I were assigned chores that needed to be completed to receive our allowance. It taught us the value of money. It didn't grow on trees, it had to be earned. We both also had savings accounts at a bank where we would make deposits and watch our savings grow. For some reason it still stays with me that at one point I managed to save $33.00 and that made me feel so proud. To me it was a million dollars.

One money lesson that will stay with me forever was when my parents were saving to build a house in the suburbs. Every penny mattered. As a family, we knew there would be no extras until Papa and Nannie reached their savings goal. They would often report how much was in the "new house" savings fund so we felt a part of the process and could see their progress. Nannie would set incremental goals. Sometimes when they reached a goal, we would get a small family treat to celebrate. Nannie and Papa finally achieved their goal and their home on Delano Street (now Homestead Avenue) in Fairhaven, Massachusetts, became the fulfillment of a hard-earned dream. This home in the suburbs created a whole new life of opportunities for our family.

One of the people I most admired in her ability to handle money was Gigi (Jean Foster), Grandad's mother. She lived modestly, was very disciplined in her savings and spending, and kept meticulous financial records. Although she was a divorcee and single mother, she was able to send both her boys to college and purchase her own home. She had the money to live a much more glamorous life but chose to live beneath her means. I remember conversations with her where she expressed her concern that Grandad and I needed a "nest egg" to fall back on in retirement. She worried that our job as ministers did not provide a pension. Because of Gigi's wisdom with money, we, and Grandad's brother Uncle Ronnie and his wife, have been blessed.

Eugenia "Jean" Foster

Not having formal training from my parents in handling money, I still pursue more knowledge. One important financial principle Grandad and I have implemented in our lives is tithing. Whatever comes into our home, the Lord gets the first 10%. This is biblical, although some people might think it foolish. Having experienced the blessings of the Lord, we would never NOT tithe. The Bible says,

"Bring the whole tithe into the storehouse, that there may be food in my house. Test me in this," says the Lord Almighty, "and see if I will not throw open the floodgates of heaven and pour out so much blessing that there will not be room enough to store it." (Malachi 3:10)

Whatever amount we have given has always come back multiplied. God's economy is so different from the world's economy. If you are faithful to give, you will receive in abundance. Our faithfulness with God's money has been key. You noticed Nana said —"God's money?" I say this because everything we have belongs to God. Isn't it wonderful God only requires we give Him back 10% and we get to keep 90% of what He has given to us?

Money, my grandchildren, will play an important part in providing a stable peaceful life. But to live peacefully, you must have a healthy attitude toward it. 1 Timothy 6:10 says, "The love of money is the root of all evil." Money in and of itself is not evil, but the "love" of money is. If we set our lives to pursue and obtain great riches, our lives will be very shallow and disappointing. There is nothing on this side of heaven money can buy that will go with us when we die. It is wise not to get caught up in the worldly pursuit of material riches, but to pursue God and the plans and purposes He has created just for you. When you pursue God and honor Him with your tithe, He will always take care of you and pour out blessings you could never have imagined.

Your grandparents are living proof of God's goodness and mercy. God sent our daughters to the best schools and provided beyond what we could have ever imagined. Always be obedient to God's Word in the managing of your finances and you shall always be provided for far beyond your expectations. Do not set your focus on money but set your focus on God.

Love you with all my heart. You, my grandchildren, are so very precious to me.

All my love,
Nana

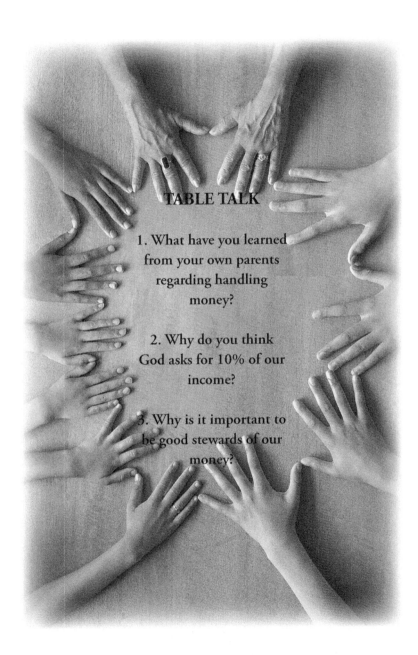

TABLE TALK

1. What have you learned from your own parents regarding handling money?

2. Why do you think God asks for 10% of our income?

3. Why is it important to be good stewards of our money?

18

The Spirit of Joy

The power of joy manifests itself within you and positively
flows through you to impact others

The prospect of the righteous is joy, but the hopes of the wicked come to nothing.
—Proverbs 10:28

Whenever someone from my father's side of the family got sick, my grandmother was immediately notified. She wasn't a doctor or nurse, but she was a fantastic cook. My nana would immediately bake a single-layered yellow sponge cake, cut it in half, and spread vanilla cream throughout the layer. It was her "version" of the popular Boston cream pie. Nana claimed the simple cake would help with the healing process. She would deliver the cake, hand it to whomever was under the weather and say, "It's just for you." It made us feel quite special. Something about that delicious cake, at the very least, had the power to heal one's spirit, if not their body. When sick—call Nana Lopes!

Recipe #18: Nana Lopes' Cream Cake (pg. 151)

My Dear Grandchildren,

My prayer is for you to experience great joy in this life. May the spirit of joy overtake you as you choose to walk in righteousness. Joy has power! It not only causes you to feel happy and satisfied, but will have a wonderfully infectious impact upon those around you.

One of the most joyful people I have ever encountered was my paternal grandmother, Linda Fermino Lopes. She was a diminutive woman who always had a good word to speak, love to give, and joy flowing from her heart. Not only was she beautiful on the inside, but she was a beauty on the outside. Although she was a simple woman, my nana enjoyed life to the fullest. She loved people and had a way of making everyone feel like they were the most important person in the world. Because of this attribute, people gravitated to her and loved being in her presence. Nana Lopes always had something for those who visited —two cookies accompanied by tea, a slice of her Boston cream cake, or a bowl of her delicious clam chowder. No matter what time of day someone stopped to visit, it was as though she had been waiting for them. Nana's simplicity, coupled with love and joy, refreshed all who knew her.

When I look at Nana Lopes' life, I realize much of what she possessed came from her relationship with God. She was a praying woman who trusted God at His word. She believed He would always take care of her and her family and often displayed this through her extreme thoughtfulness and selfless generosity. Whether it was the second-hand clothes Nana passed on from the wealthy family she worked for or the home-baked cookies straight from the oven, or the bouquet of freshly picked daffodils from her garden,

Linda Fermino Lopes

Nana Lopes always had a gift with which to bless others.

I could always depend on her being the same—joyful and at peace. No matter what was happening, Nana maintained her focus on the Lord. Today's Bible verse says the prospect of the righteous is joy, but the hopes of the wicked come to nothing. Nana Lopes' life taught me that being in a right relationship with God is one of the most important things

78

we can pursue. This righteous relationship brings overflowing joy and allows us to navigate the difficult times that will come our way.

At times, Nana's life was challenging due to her and Grandpa's limited financial means. Grandpa Lopes was a longshoreman who worked sporadically, and Nana was a housekeeper who worked three days a week. Although their finances were limited, they managed to live a life filled with joy and abundance. Nana could take a little and make it into something extravagant! I always loved the edible Easter candy centerpieces she would make on beautiful antique platters.

Nana Lopes experienced some very difficult times—the loss of a twenty-something-year-old brother by an explosion on a ship he worked on, and the loss of three other brothers in their early fifties from sudden heart attacks. Through it all, my grandmother remained steadfast in her walk with the Lord and joyful in her spirit. The Lord used her joy to overflow and touch our lives in a beautiful way. Not only was the joy of the Lord her strength, but it flowed to those who were connected to her. Her joyful spirit taught me that "joy is a choice." We can choose to rejoice and trust God in all things, or we can let life weigh us down.

My beloved grandchildren, may you choose the Lord every day, opening your heart to a spirit of joy. Your life will be much fuller and richer because of it. May the joy of the Lord be your strength.

All my love,
Nana

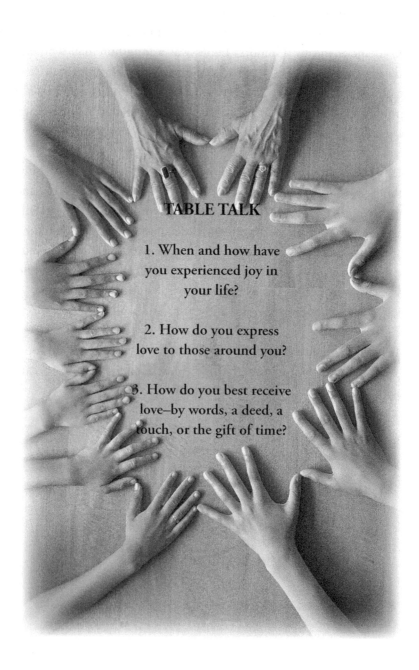

TABLE TALK

1. When and how have
you experienced joy in
your life?

2. How do you express
love to those around you?

3. How do you best receive
love–by words, a deed, a
touch, or the gift of time?

19

A Good Name

An honorable name opens doors and creates a legacy of blessings

A good name is more desirable than great riches; to be esteemed is better than silver or gold. —Proverbs 22:1

Back in my elementary school days, students were dismissed from school at noon to take the short walk home, eat lunch, and then return to school. My parents worked opposite shifts. So, it was my dad's duty to prepare our daily lunch. One of my favorite lunches that Dad served was store-bought chicken pot pie. I loved them. It wasn't 'til I became an adult that I had the pleasure of eating homemade chicken pot pie made by my husband's grandmother, Myrtle Christian. Now that's some real comfort food. Not only is it delicious, but it brings back the warmest of memories.

Recipe #19: Nana Christian's Chicken Pot Pie (pg. 152)

My Dear Grandchildren,

One person who has earned a "good" name in this life here on earth is your great-grandfather, my dad, Anthony "Jep" Lopes. The great-grandchildren who were fortunate to know and remember him, called him "Papa." We pronounced it "puppa." Papa was a soft-spoken gentleman who was a friend to all.

It was a privilege to be brought up in the small town of Fairhaven, Massachusetts where Papa had

Anthony "Jep" Lopes

been a local sports hero. He was known by many for his exceptional sports records in basketball, football, baseball, and track. As excellent of an athlete as Papa was, he was known even more for his honorable ways. Often when meeting local adults, their faces would light up and they'd immediately ask, "Are you Jeppy's daughter?" Sensing that people loved and respected my father elicited pride in me. As a byproduct of Papa's good reputation in the community, I was often granted favor—from getting my first job to making the cheerleading squad. Doors were opened for me because of Papa's good name.

Although Papa was not a church-going person, he believed in God and prayed daily. His life was guided by spiritual principles. He lived his life in such a way that made it clear to everyone who knew him the high value he placed on relationships. Family always came first. Papa demonstrated this in many sacrificial ways. As children, Uncle Carl and I often accompanied Papa to visit his homebound elderly relatives. The visits were a way of showing them respect, honor, and love. Even as a child, the pride Papa had in his children was very evident. When his relatives made mention of us, Papa would beam with pride. We knew we were truly loved.

Papa always demonstrated loyalty and commitment to family and friends. He and Nannie were married for 62 years, and they left a wonderful legacy and example of what marriage looks like when a couple vows for "better or for worse." His faithfulness as a husband and father created a solid foundation for his children, and even his grandchildren.

A few years before Papa passed away, we had one of our many "reminiscing" talks. Papa shared, "I did the best I knew to be a good husband and father. I may not have always hit the mark, but one thing I can say is that I was faithful to both my wife and my children."

This touched me deeply because we live in a time when everyone seems to be out for themselves and commitment to marital vows is taken very lightly. Let your Papa's faithful example be carried on by you, my dear grandchildren.

Papa worked hard to maintain a good name. Because of his good name, everyone in his family benefited. As you go through life always remember that your "name" and the reputation associated with it will have a ripple effect. In other words, they will have an impact on the way that you and those whom you love are treated. If you live your life honoring Jesus, you will leave a legacy of blessings. I thank the Lord for having given me an honorable father like Papa.

All my love,
Nana

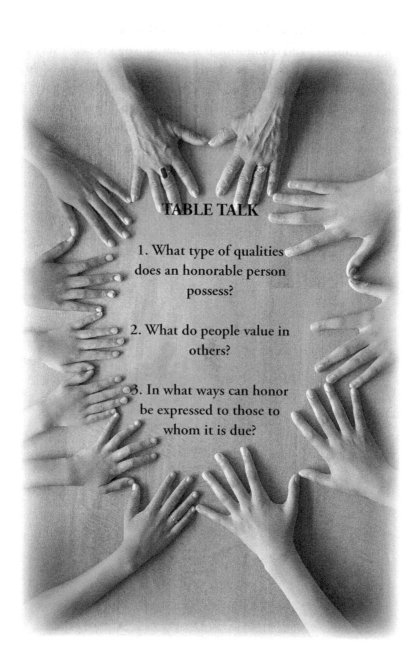

TABLE TALK

1. What type of qualities does an honorable person possess?

2. What do people value in others?

3. In what ways can honor be expressed to those to whom it is due?

20

Be Diligent

Diligence has the ability to positively affect your destiny

I went past the field of a sluggard, past the vineyard of someone who has no sense; thorns had come up everywhere, the ground was covered with weeds, and the stone wall was in ruins. I applied my heart to what I observed and learned a lesson from what I saw: A little sleep, a little slumber, a little folding of the hands to rest— and poverty will come on you like a thief and scarcity like an armed man. —Proverbs 24:30-34

Grandad and I recently began trying our hand at gardening in a little 5'x10' plot at our local community garden. We now know (the hard way) that diligent soil preparation, weeding, and watering are necessary to have a bountiful harvest. As in many areas of life, fruitfulness and diligence go hand in hand.

One of our more successful garden crops has been yellow summer squash. We enjoy it sautéed with onions.

Recipe #20: Sautéed Yellow Summer Squash (pg. 152)

My Dear Grandchildren,

In the above verses, God speaks through the writer about the perils of a lazy person. The writer begins by describing a neglected, overgrown vineyard. Only weeds and thorns were thriving where there should have been overflowing grapes. He goes on to suggest that if we are lazy, poverty will overtake us. If we want to be fruitful and have what we need in life, we must be diligent to work hard and put forth our best efforts in everything we pursue.

You, my grandchildren, are blessed to have wonderful examples of hard-working ancestors on both sides of your family. In your lineage, as far back as your great-great grandparents, there are longshoremen, merchant marine sailors, factory seamstresses, policemen, nurses, machinists, bookkeepers, marketing consultants, businesswomen, business managers, teachers, home-makers, housekeepers, and pastors who all displayed diligence.

You come from people who desired to progress and worked hard so that their children would reap the benefits and do better than they did. Most of your ancestors who immigrated, came from the Caribbean or the Cape Verde Islands to the United States in search of a better life. All of you have an assortment of ancestors who either came here as immigrants or slaves. All of them had challenging circumstances. Through diligence, they overcame.

Diligence means putting our best effort into whatever task we are pursuing. Being diligent and industrious are virtues worthy of respect. In whatever you pursue, do it to the best of your ability and trust God to make the outcome better than your abilities alone could ever accomplish. Wherever you are and whatever you put your hands to, make sure when you leave the place it is BETTER because you have been there.

God wants to be acknowledged in all we do and in every area of our lives. Our hard work glorifies Him and will often elevate us to higher places. Take pride in the work you do; work in a spirit of excellence. Do not be lazy, my dear grandchild, because laziness will only dishonor God and lead to poverty.

As a young child, I remember the diligence exercised by my parents in building a new home for us in the suburbs. My father worked every day from 8:00 am-3:30 pm helping to physically build the house. At 4:00 pm, he'd start his factory job that ended at midnight. In essence, he worked 16-hour days, five days a week. On weekends, he and my mom would spend the entire weekend working together on the house. He maintained the same routine for several months until the house was completed. Papa saved thousands of dollars by providing that labor. Physically, he lost several pounds because of his hectic schedule. Papa's desire to provide a better life for his family kept him faithful to see the job through to completion. Because of my par-

"Jep" and Jan Lopes

ents' diligence, their children got a great education and were exposed to many new life experiences. We thank God for their sacrifice.

Papa (Jep) Lopes and Nannie (Jan), my parents, always encouraged their children to work in a spirit of excellence and to take pride in whatever we put our hands to, no matter how prestigious or mundane the task might have been. They'd then go on to say if you're going to be a teacher, be the best teacher you can be. If you're going to be a garbage man, be the best one there is. My dear children, take pride in the job or career God gives you and let your performance be superb. If your mindset is to do everything unto the glory of God, you will be consistently motivated to give every task your all and do it in excellence. Keep in the forefront of your mind, you represent God, your heavenly Father. Someone may want to come into a relationship with God because of how you represented Him in your work ethic. Your diligence points to your character. Let your character speak volumes of who you are in Christ Jesus. If you put forth your best effort, poverty will not "come upon you like a thief." Instead, you will live to enjoy the fruit of your labor.

All my love,
Nana

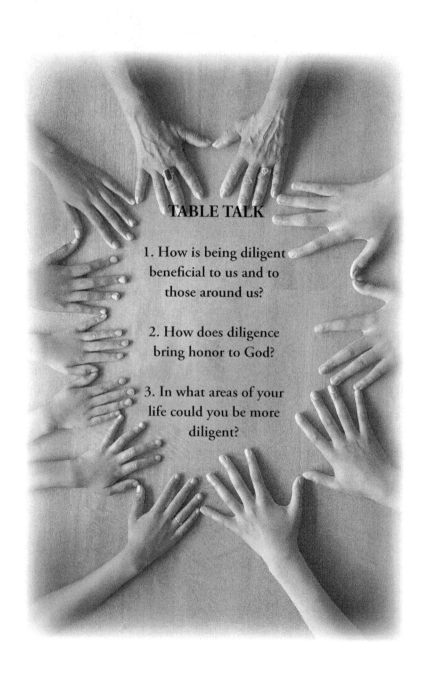

TABLE TALK

1. How is being diligent beneficial to us and to those around us?

2. How does diligence bring honor to God?

3. In what areas of your life could you be more diligent?

21

Honesty, God's Requirement

We walk in honesty and integrity to demonstrate who God
is in our lives and to the world

The Lord detests lying lips, but delights in people who are trustworthy.
—Proverbs 12:22

There are times when the truth is difficult to hear and may not be what we want to hear, but it's exactly what we need to hear. No one wants to hear someone tell them, "Wow, your breath is really bad today!" And yet, the person who had the courage to tell us that truth was really doing us (and everyone else we might breathe upon) a big favor.

Timing is important when we need to share a difficult truth with someone. You want to help them, not destroy them. You don't want to tell them at a moment when others are around. The point is to bless them, not embarrass them. You don't want to tell them when they are already at a very low point emotionally and may not be able to handle "one more thing!" You'll know when the time is right. If you genuinely care about the person, you'll understand the why, how, and when you tell them a difficult truth is even more important than what you want to tell them.

Timing is everything! Here is a recipe involving some very precise timing in its preparation. For a very special treat, you'll enjoy this recipe for Prime Rib.

Recipe #21: Prime Rib Roast (pg. 153)

My Dear Grandchildren,

The language of God is the language of truth. His desire is that we all speak the language of truth fluently and consistently.

Proverbs 12:22 tells us the Lord hates lying lips but delights in people who are trustworthy. Trust can never be fully earned by people who bend the truth or tell outright lies. You will be tested in this area. There will be times when you will need to choose between lying to keep yourself from getting into hot water or modeling Jesus by telling the truth. May you always make the decision to honor God with truthfulness. People who cannot be trusted to be honest are people who typically have poor relationships with others. The life of a person of integrity displays honesty and models God's Word by their lifestyle. Choose to be strong; choose to be truthful.

There are a few reasons Nana believes honesty is so very important. There are many languages spoken throughout the earth, but the language of God supersedes them all; truth is a powerful force. Honesty and truth set us apart as people who belong to God.

God's character and His Word require that we walk in honesty to exemplify who He is to unbelievers. You do harm to the kingdom of God when you say you are a Christian and then act dishonestly with others. Secondly, honesty enables others to respect and trust you. If others can trust you, perhaps they will come to see Christ who is in you, and even desire to come to know Him personally. Then, they too, will experience the abundant life He has so graciously provided to those who believe in Him.

Lastly, honesty is a character trait that affects many areas of your life from your relationships and careers to personal and spiritual growth. If you walk in integrity and honesty, every area of your life stands to be positively impacted and improved. Your relationships with others will thrive because they will find you credible. Your personal life will be at peace because you will be modeling what Christ has demonstrated. Your spiritual life will flourish because you are putting into practice what God's Word has taught you. Integrity and honesty also create and maintain a fertile spiritual environment where God can manifest Himself.

For the people of God, to be fully honest requires that what we believe, say, and do, are in alignment with God and His Word. We are not fully honest with ourselves and others unless all three aspects are in sync. As your grandmother, my prayer is for you to always choose truth and honesty. If you do, God will go before you in ways you could never have imagined. Be honest, be blessed, and be a blessing to others. You can't go wrong with the truth.

All my love,
Nana

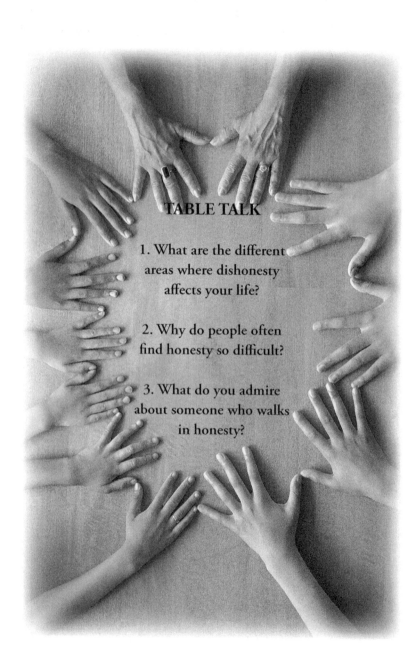

TABLE TALK

1. What are the different areas where dishonesty affects your life?

2. Why do people often find honesty so difficult?

3. What do you admire about someone who walks in honesty?

22

Embrace your Heritage

Accept and embrace your cultural heritage

The Lord will make you the head, not the tail. If you pay attention to the commands of the Lord your God that I give you this day and carefully follow them, you will always be at the top, never at the bottom.
—Deuteronomy 28:13

My maternal great-grandfather (Nannie's grandfather) did not come to the United States of his own volition. At fourteen years old he was shanghaied by a fishing boat passing through the Cape Verde Islands. As he helped to load the ship, the crew locked him in and sailed off to sea. The ship landed in Provincetown, Massachusetts and my great-grandfather eventually made his way to New Bedford, Massachusetts where there was a large Cape Verdean population. When he contacted his family in the Cape Verde Islands, they wanted nothing to do with him because they thought he had intentionally run away from home. This caused a vast riff in his family that lasted over 20 years. He eventually settled down and married my great-grandmother.

His daughter Aurora, my maternal grandmother, had a recipe for a better life. It was to gather the extended family at her summer cottage for good food and a refreshing swim. My favorite recipe of Nana Pereira's was her Summer Jag.

Recipe #22: Summer Jag (Cape Verdean rice and beans) with Butternut Squash and Kale (pg. 154)

Aurora Pereira

93

My Dear Grandchildren,

Be appreciative of your rich cultural and racial heritage. The conditions that brought your ancestors to the United States speak of unique sets of trials and triumphs that preceded your birth. A kidnap victim, slaves and immigrants from Africa, Europe, Guyana, and Jamaica. Both sides of your maternal grandfather's family, reportedly have Native American ancestors who were already here when all the others arrived. We honor them all.

The beauty of the body of Christ is we all have a transcending spiritual ancestry uniting every believer in Christ. It does not mean you should negate or minimize your natural heritage. God so loved the [whole] world that He gave His only begotten son. . . (John 3:16). To ponder and value the origins of the blood that flows in your veins should only increase your appreciation for the power of God to connect us to those with very different stories than our own.

And yet, it is a harsh reality that in life there may be those who seek to discount or dismiss your existence based solely upon your race or ethnicity. They may hate your blackness, or your whiteness. Rise above, dear ones. Stand up for justice for all people and insist upon it for yourself.

No one and nothing can stop the plans and purposes God has ordained for your life. If you have chosen to walk with God, your destiny and life are in His hands. Walk in God's favor and doors will open for you. Go through life confidently, knowing God is with you and for you. If God is for us, who can be against us? (Romans 8:31)

Yes, in life you will have both challenges and challengers, but if you place your faith in God, you will ultimately be victorious and accomplish all God has for your life. It's important for me to emphasize God's plans must become your plans. We cannot go on a self-charted course through life and expect God to move on our behalf. If you are walking out God's plan, no one will be able to hinder you.

You stand with God, who will never leave you nor forsake you, and on the shoulders of many generations of ancestral predecessors who overcame great odds to prevail. Both sets of your ancestors worked hard, valued education, handled their money wisely, and when possible, invested in homes of their own. From the immigration of my great-grandparents from the Cape Verde Islands, or your fathers' parents from Guyana or Jamaica, to your parents' generation, each generation has done better than the last in the areas of education and finances. Each generation sacrificed for the next generation. You, my dear grandchildren, have been given a leg up in life. Use your advantage wisely.

The following was written in the Old Testament to the Israelites who had been the object of ethnic and spiritual oppression in their time. If we too walk in obedience to the Lord, the same overcoming power and benefits will be bestowed upon us.

"The Lord will establish you as his holy people, as he promised you on oath, if you keep the commands of the Lord your God and walk in obedience to him. Then all the peoples on earth will see that you are called by the name of the Lord, and they will fear you. The Lord will grant you abundant prosperity—in the fruit of your womb, the young of your livestock and the crops of your ground—in the land he swore to your ancestors to give you. The Lord will open the heavens, the storehouse of his bounty, to send rain on your land in season and to bless all the work of your hands. You will lend to many nations but will borrow from none. The Lord will make you the head, not the tail. If you pay attention to the commands of the Lord your God that I give you this day and carefully follow them, you will always be at the top, never at the bottom. Do not turn aside from any of the commands I give you today, to the right or to the left, following other gods and serving them." (Deuteronomy 28:9-14)

You will overcome every form of bias against you, and even prosper, if you follow the Lord in obedience. The journey will have its twists and turns, but the victory will ultimately be yours. Be encouraged, my dear grandchildren, you will be more than conquerors.

All my love,
Nana

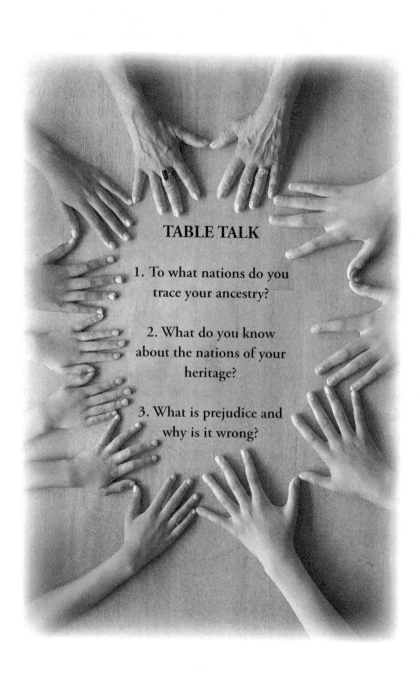

TABLE TALK

1. To what nations do you
trace your ancestry?

2. What do you know
about the nations of your
heritage?

3. What is prejudice and
why is it wrong?

RELATIONAL LIFE LESSONS

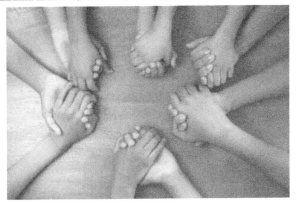

23

The Importance of a Strong Family

A healthy family provides stability and strength from one
generation to the next

*Love the Lord your God with all your heart and with all your soul and with
all your strength. These commandments that I give you today are to be on your
hearts. Impress them on your children. Talk about them when you sit at home
and when you walk along the road, when you lie down and when you get up.*
—Deuteronomy 6:5-7

One of my greatest sources of joy is watching my grandchildren interact
with one another. Yes, they sometimes squabble, but more often than
not, they look out for each other. They are protective and loving to their
siblings which warms my heart.

I still remember the day I realized my older brother loved me and would
forever protect me. I was about five and he was about eight years old. It was a
snowy winter day, and we were out in our yard having a snowball fight with
my brother's closest friend. My brother's friend at one point intentionally
threw a snowball that hit me in the face. Anger rose up in my brother as
he confronted his friend with a barrage of snowballs while yelling, "You
better never do that to my sister again." After that burst of anger, my brother
promptly took me by the hand and led me into the house. I remember
thinking, "My brother really likes me!" My brother and I have remained close
throughout the years, always in one another's corner. There is much power
in the sibling relationship. May your relationships with your brothers and
sisters always remain sweet, yet strong, like this delicious recipe of Nannie's
Gingersnap Cookies.

Recipe #23: Nannie's Gingersnap Cookies (pg. 154)

My Dear Grandchildren,

God established families as a tool to provide nurture, love, and connection. And yet, over the years there has been a breakdown and disintegration in overall family life. Many families are not functioning as God intended. The increase of dysfunctional families has negatively impacted our entire society. There are some ways in which families can and should be a blessing, as well as basic things we need to do to keep our families healthy and connected.

Times have changed since the 1950s and 60s when I was a child. Growing up, my family would gather around the dinner table on a nightly basis. My mom insisted that no matter where we were or what we were doing, we needed to be home in time for dinner. Our meals were simple and often consisted of leftovers that we'd eat for days on end, but that did not matter. What mattered was that we were around the table talking and sharing with one another.

John B. Lopes

On a regular basis, my paternal grandfather, Johnny Lopes, would come over during dinner and sit on the outskirts of our kitchen table. He rarely ate with us but came by just to be part of our conversations. We were sure to be entertained when he was there because he told the best stories—some true and others straight out of his imagination. Grandpa Lopes was a character. Most of the time the conversations around the dinner table were lighthearted and fun, but there were times when arguments erupted, and tears were shed. My dad, Papa, always made sure that by the time we cleared the table everyone was at peace.

It was at the dinner table we learned to address difficult things head on. We experienced what a family was and how we all needed to support one another. We learned what love was and saw what it looked like in action. We learned to be grateful to God in all things. Although my parents weren't church-going Christians until my teen years, in my early years we never started a meal without giving thanks to God for His provision. It may seem small and insignificant, but this act of thanksgiving kept me keenly aware that God loved us and provided for us. Our daily dinner connection gave

God an opportunity to work within our family relationships and create a strong foundation that has been carried on to the next generation.

Today, many family relationships are being threatened by busy schedules, financial pressures, divorce, and technology in the form of cell phones, video games, computers, and TVs just to name a few. We have grown so affluent as a country that nearly everyone has their own TV, laptop computer, and cell phone in their own room. Many families reside in the same house but do not actually "do" life together. Their lives are not relational or emotionally connected. God intended for the family unit to be an equipping entity that would teach, mold, shape, and provide love to its members. Family was meant to be a place of security and protection. We were meant to love each other and share life in a meaningful way with God always at the very center.

My dear grandchildren, as you grow older, you'll increasingly realize how your relationship with God and your family have the most influence on your happiness. Worship God and esteem your family. The love and time you pour into your immediate family will someday come back to bless you abundantly. Spend time with your mom and dad—you might be surprised at how much they actually know and how much they love you. Likewise, love your brothers and sisters. Friends will come and go throughout your lives, but your siblings will remain constant. Yes, there will be times when they will get on your last nerve, but they will also be a blessing. Appreciate the gift God has given you in the form of your family.

The opening scripture admonishes us to teach our children about God's way. If we commit to serving our families, we will stay on a path that will strengthen and build them up. Let's make our family a priority in our hearts and purpose to stay emotionally close to each other no matter where we live or how old we get. You, my dear ones, are so very blessed to come from a healthy stable family, one that values and loves you. Be a blessing and pass it forward.

All my love,
Nana

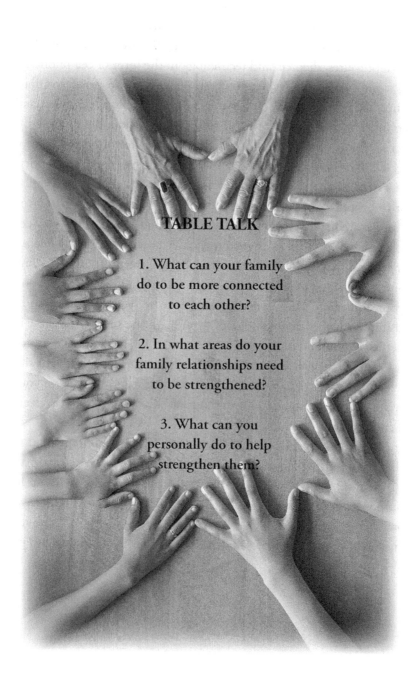

TABLE TALK

1. What can your family do to be more connected to each other?

2. In what areas do your family relationships need to be strengthened?

3. What can you personally do to help strengthen them?

24

Honor Your Parents

Two important biblical promises and benefits to those who
honor their parents

Children, obey your parents in the Lord, for this is right. "Honor
your father and mother"—which is the first commandment with a
promise—"so that it may go well with you and that you may enjoy a
long life on the earth." —Ephesians 6:1-3

Old pictures can bring a wide range of emotions. When I look back at Thanksgiving and Christmas pictures going back over the course of my lifetime, it's always a marvel to note how time has changed the lineup of those seated around the table. In the span of time from when I was a little girl seated at the "kids table" to now, in my latest role as "Nana," the cast of family characters has changed dramatically. There have been plenty of cast changes as new faces have been added, the little ones from back then have all grown up, the young adults have gotten old. Those who were elderly, have gone home to be with Jesus. All we have of those who have gone ahead of us are our memories of their persona, recollection of the sound of their laughter, and in some cases, the special recipes they brought to our table.

I'd like to remember and honor the memory of my Aunt Ethel with this recipe for her Chocolate Torte. It brings a smile to my face as I think of how blessed I am to have had her in my life. And her food? I can almost taste it. My dear, sweet auntie, this is for you!

Recipe #24: Aunt Ethel's Chocolate Torte (pg. 155)

My Dear Grandchildren,

You are so very fortunate to have been blessed with parents who truly desired to have children. They love you dearly. It is a gift from God to have loving parents that daily prove their love by sacrificing for your good. For Grandad and Nana, it has been both a joy and blessing to behold. As a Christian grandmother, I certainly believe children are a gift from God, but also think good parents are a blessing from above. Never take your parents for granted but live with a spirit of gratitude for these two "gifts" God has bestowed upon you. Regardless of the level of material wealth you may possess in your lifetime, you have already inherited great riches in the form of your parents who love you.

The Bible commands us to honor our parents so life may go well with us, and we will live a long life. This is a commandment with a promise. (Ephesians 6:2-3). If we do one thing, another thing will happen. If we honor our parents, our lives will go well, and we will enjoy a long life.

What does it mean to honor someone? To honor someone is to hold them in high regard, to feel they have high value and are deserving of our respect. Your parents are to be honored, both while they are young and when they have grown old, whether you agree or disagree with their decisions. No one will care for your well-being and love you as deeply as they do. As a young person, it will be difficult to understand the depth of your parents' love, but trust me, they love you deeply and always want the best for you. Unfortunately, many people fail to recognize the extent of their parents' love until they are grown and have children of their own. Prayerfully, you will come to such an understanding and appreciation while you are still young.

What does honor look like? Sometimes it looks like obedience. Honor your parents by being obedient to them and to the Word of God. Your parents are not perfect, but neither is anyone else. Your parents will make mistakes, but remember they are doing the best they can with the knowledge they possess. Your parents trust God and assuredly He will correct them if need be. Even when you disagree with your parents, choose to honor them by being lovingly obedient.

Honor can also take the shape of pleasing your parents by making them proud. You honor your parents when you excel in school, or when you express your gratitude for something they've done for you or simply by wanting to spend time with them. Nothing makes a parent prouder than to see their children implementing the godly principles they have been taught.

Even when you become an adult, continue to honor your parents. They will need you more than you'll ever know. Call to let them know you love them; it will bring them such joy. It will also be your responsibility to take care of them when they can no longer take care of themselves. Let it be an honor to lovingly care for them. Both Nana and Grandad had the privilege of taking care of their elderly parents. It taught us so much about life. We were honored to have had that opportunity. When our parents transitioned to be with the Lord, we were left with gratitude for the precious time we spent with them.

Nana and Grandad want you all to live a long and prosperous life to the glory of God. What does the Word of God say? "Honor your parents and you shall live a long life." You are a reflection of your parents, so let your light shine brightly.

All my love,
Nana

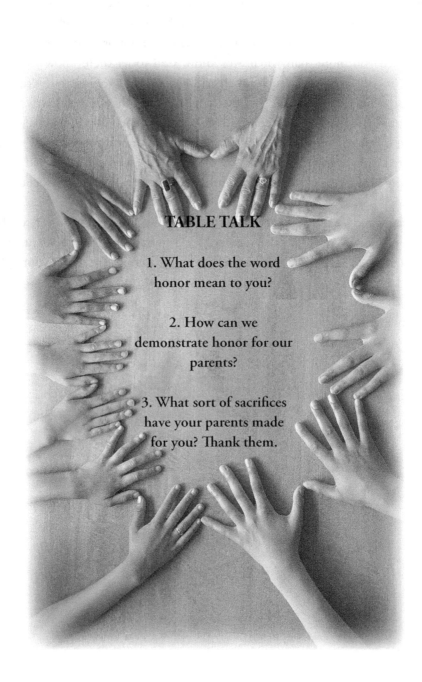

TABLE TALK

1. What does the word honor mean to you?

2. How can we demonstrate honor for our parents?

3. What sort of sacrifices have your parents made for you? Thank them.

25

Sow Kindness

Never underestimate how one simple act of kindness can
change someone's life

Anxiety weighs down the heart, but a kind word cheers it up. —Proverbs 12:25

Valentine's Day recently passed, and I was under the weather and unable to see my family. The week after Valentine's Day, my youngest daughter came by for a visit with my two granddaughters. As they were taking off their coats I noticed my granddaughter Makena, the youngest of the two girls, had her hand tightly fisted. Once her coat was off, she walked over to me and opened her hand to reveal five or six wrapped chocolate hearts. She quietly said, "Nana, I saved these for you because I know how much you like chocolate." You could have blown me over with the joy I felt. I could not have received a more thoughtful and loving gift. Her sweet kindness will remain in my heart forever.

Aunt Juju often presented each of us with a box of her delicious homemade fudge at Christmas. May Auntie Juju's recipe of Creamy Holiday Fudge also add some sweet kindness to your life.

Recipe #25: Juju's Creamy Holiday Fudge (pg. 155)

My Dear Grandchildren,

Nana and Grandad pray for you each and every day. We often pray God will place a hedge of protection around you in every aspect of your life and that you will be both recipients and vessels of kindness in this harsh world. We are living in a spiritually darkened era—a world much crueler than the one in which we grew up. Our world seems to have no regard for an individual's well-being. Rudeness and callousness seem to reign on social media and in politics. It grieves me to see how political leaders who should be exemplary, are often slanderous and heartless.

At some point in our lives, we will all be faced with hardships and difficulties. In those times, wouldn't it be wonderful to hear an encouraging word or have kindness extended to us? Many of us have become much too self-absorbed in our own lives to even think of extending ourselves to others. As Christians, we are called to be God-centered. When we live a God-focused life, we are cognizant that our lives exist to glorify God. If we purposely conduct ourselves in a God-centered way, in the midst of every situation, we should ask ourselves the following questions: "What would Jesus do?" "What would He say?" "How would Jesus treat this person?" "How should I respond and react?" "What would bring God glory?"

Always treat people with the same kindness you would like extended to you. In Matthew 7:12 (often referred to as the "Golden Rule") the Bible says, ". . .do to others what you would have them do to you. . ." Kindness costs us nothing but pays great dividends. We often do not know the turmoil another person may be going through. Sometimes just a kind word, an affirming smile, or a gentle pat on the arm can lift a person's spirit. God desires us to become His vessels of love and kindness in this often, harsh world. Let God's love flow through you to touch someone else's life.

When Nana was a 12-year-old junior high school student, she sat in her homeroom behind a boy named Joe. Joe was a very tall, handsome boy who was considered to be one of the tough, cool kids. Kids were respectful but intimidated by him. Every morning Joe would turn around and talk to me. As we got to know one another, I sensed things were not well in his family life and it had to do with his stepfather. Because of his home situation, Joe often had not completed his homework. Nana would ask him about his homework every morning and then proceed to help him to get it done. After two years,

Joe left my junior high to attend a different school and we rarely saw each other.

About 35 years later at Nana's 30th high school class reunion, Joe showed up. I was surprised to see him since he hadn't graduated with my class. Joe shared with me that he came to the reunion just to thank me for the kindness extended to him when we were in junior high. He went on to say that it had been the most difficult time in his life and his stepfather often beat his mom and him. Nana's friendship and kindness during that period of his life kept him sane. Nana had no idea the extent of Joe's pain and situation, but God did. God used Nana's kindness as a light in someone else's life.

We may never know what people are going through and because of that we should choose kindness when dealing with others. The Bible verse used for this devotion says, "Anxiety weighs down the heart, but a kind word cheers it up." May you, my blessed grandchildren, be the ones to speak that kind word. Be kind, even if it makes you unpopular to some, it will make you a favorite of others.

Be sure to extend your kindness at home. It is important to show kindness to your siblings and family members, not just to friends and acquaintances. Always remember, the Bible says, "We reap what we sow"—so sow what is good. Please know that your kindness pleases God, and it makes both your parents and grandparents so very proud of you. We love you to the moon, and back. . . and then some. Show and sow God's kindness.

All my love,
Nana

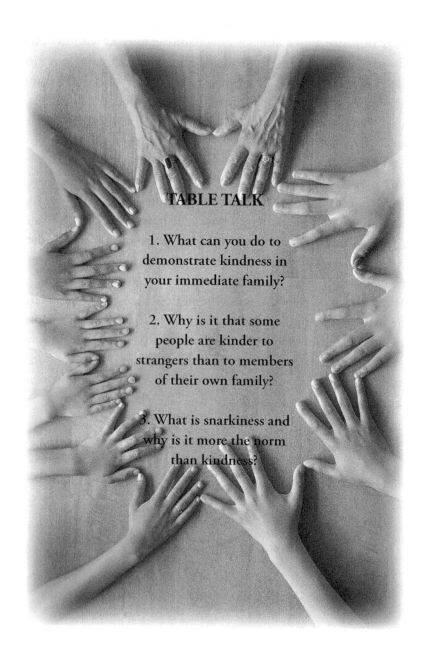

TABLE TALK

1. What can you do to demonstrate kindness in your immediate family?

2. Why is it that some people are kinder to strangers than to members of their own family?

3. What is snarkiness and why is it more the norm than kindness?

26

Choosing the Right Friends

The right friends will enhance your life and enable you to
remain on a righteous path

*The righteous choose their friends carefully, but the way of the wicked leads them
astray. —Proverbs 12:26*

Recently, Grandad and I attended a most wonderful potluck luncheon. Many of the attendees were from places other than the USA, and the menu was reflective of our diversity. Among the dishes we shared were chicken biryani and samosas from India, curried chicken from Jamaica, rice and beans from Puerto Rico, and manicotti from Italy. We not only dined extraordinarily well, but thoroughly enjoyed one another's company. The whole event was a wonderful illustration of effective friendships. In true friendship, everyone brings something to the table (so to speak). It involves both giving and receiving and is enjoyable and beneficial to each participant.

No matter from what country you may trace your roots, you'll probably enjoy this recipe for Cheese Straws from Grandma Morris (in-law) from the nation of Guyana.

Recipe #26: Cheese Straws (pg. 156)

My Dear Grandchildren,

As you go through life you will have many decisions to make. Some of them will be life-changing. Among those important decisions are your choices of good friends. Depending on their character, the friends we choose can either bring "spiritual" life or death to us.

It is paramount that YOU choose your friends, do not let them choose you. Many people (all with various motives and reasons) will want to be your friend. Make sure you are the one to choose whom you will befriend. Select friends who will influence you positively and not take you off a godly course.

It is okay to have friends who are different from you, but they should possess the same core values. It is important to have sincere, good friends because those closest to us influence our thinking the most. The only influences we should allow into our lives are positive ones.

Look at potential friends and ask yourself the following questions. Do they desire to do good? Do they value hard work? Do they want to achieve everything God desires them to achieve? Are they of good character or do they cheat, lie, curse, and do whatever it takes to get their own way? Also look at your friend's behavior—are they respectful to adults and those in authority? Can they discern between good and evil?

If you align yourselves with friends that are not of good character, their negative ways will eventually begin to rub off on you. There is an old saying that says, "Birds of a feather flock together." It means people stick with people that are like themselves. People will judge you by the company you keep. The Bible puts it this way, "Do not be misled; bad company corrupts good character." (1 Corinthians 15:33) If you are close friends with kids who are up to no good, people will think you are a troublemaker too. Over time, they might be proven right.

When he was in his mid-teens, my brother Carl fell into a group of friends with whom he began to get into mischievous activities such as smoking and drinking. Thanks to concerned neighbors, one day he got caught with them. It was the best thing that ever happened. Out of tough love for Carl and for fear of the potential cost of taking it too lightly, my parents punished him severely. He had to stay at home ALL SUMMER, going no further than the yard. By the end of the summer, that group of boys had forgotten all about my brother and moved on to make other friends. I thank God Carl was forced to find a different group of friends who had values more like his own. Of course, there were those who thought the punishment was excessive, but it proved to be wise. Sadly, those friends of Uncle Carl did not fare as well. One even lost his life to drugs by the age of 27. Uncle Carl went on to become a great artist and a respected teacher, someone we are all proud of. Your friends have an influence in your life. Prayerfully, you will choose your friends wisely.

A good sincere friend will value and like you for the person you are. You will not have to compromise to win their friendship. You will be accepted by them by just being yourself. You do not need to have a whole lot of friends—two or three good friends is all anyone needs.

Remember to pick wisely when choosing friends; it is one of the more important decisions in determining whether or not you'll have an abundant life. The opening verse says, "The righteous choose their friends carefully." Be righteous and make wise decisions when choosing. A good friend is invaluable. You, my dear grandchildren, deserve to have great friends.

All my love,
Nana

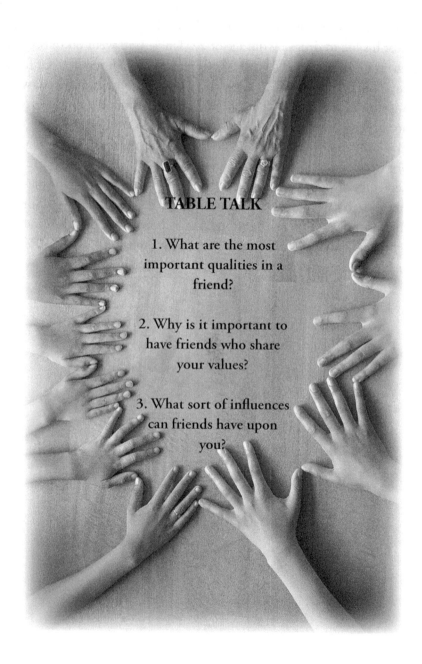

TABLE TALK

1. What are the most
important qualities in a
friend?

2. Why is it important to
have friends who share
your values?

3. What sort of influences
can friends have upon
you?

27

The Gift of Forgiveness

Learn to forgive quickly and willingly to receive love freely

Be kind and compassionate to one another, forgiving each other, just as in Christ God forgave you. —Ephesians 4:32

God has a sense of humor! I always desired to have a third child, preferably a son. In seeking God about this I heard the Holy Spirit say, "I will place him in your home!" Years went by and then suddenly, one Wednesday evening a 14-year-old boy who had been attending church with his brother approached Grandad and me. He explained that he had been kicked out of his foster home and didn't have anywhere to go. We decided to bring him home for the night and contact his social worker in the morning so she could find him a new placement.

Things did not quite work out that way. Two and a half years later, the young boy was still living with us. It was in that time period I learned how to walk in forgiveness and unconditional love. We had some very sweet and hilarious times with our "new" son, but we were also tested beyond measure by him. I remember at one point laying prostrate on the floor crying out to God that I could no longer handle the pain and havoc our son was causing. God clearly spoke to me, "If you can offer forgiveness and extend unconditional love, I'll enable him to receive and give love." Well, that was many years ago and that little boy is nearly 40 years old, a dad of three children of his own. He continues to be an integral part of our family. One of his favorite dishes is beef brisket which he jokingly calls "brisk."

Recipe #27: Fresh Beef Brisket (pg. 156)

My Dear Grandchildren,

Everyone who desires to have a fruitful Christian life must learn the importance of walking in forgiveness. In my heart, forgiveness is just as important as the subject of love—in fact, the two are entwined. We all like to think we would extend forgiveness to others. But the truth is when we are the offended party, we find it difficult to forgive. God is very clear in the Bible that we are to forgive those who have offended or hurt us. In fact, there are no exceptions.

The Bible clearly states that all mankind is born with a sinful nature. It is amazing to think while we were still sinners, Jesus Christ surrendered his life and was crucified so we could be forgiven. Let that soak in—while we were still steeped in our sins, Christ died a horrific death so we could be saved. Even when we were at odds with Him, Jesus gave up his life for us. This sacrificial act is almost incomprehensible to me. Christ died so we could be forgiven—what an extraordinary act of love.

The Bible tells us we should "be kind and compassionate to one another, forgiving each other, just as in Christ, God forgave you" (Ephesians 4:32). When we grasp the truth of Christ forgiving our sins and even dying on the cross on our behalf, it eliminates any justification we may have for holding on to unforgiveness toward those who have offended us. We are told to extend forgiveness to all people including the person who broke your heart, the friend who betrayed you, or the person who may have tried to violate you —everyone. Jesus states in Matthew 6, "For if you forgive other people when they sin against you, your heavenly Father will also forgive you. But if you do not forgive others their sins, your Father will not forgive your sins" (Matthew 6:14-15). Not one of us can afford to be at odds with God.

One thing for sure is that unforgiveness usually hurts only one person and it's the person who decides not to forgive. Holding an offense is the trick of the enemy and is meant to bind, hinder, and embitter a person. There are times we become offended, and the other person doesn't even realize they have offended us. We justify our unforgiveness because we are hurt. There are also times when a person may intentionally try to hurt or harm us, but we are still required by God to forgive them. If Satan can keep us offended and unable to forgive, then he has us precisely where we do not ever want to be—out of relationship with Christ. When we extend forgiveness, it keeps us free and in communion with God.

Although forgiveness is a must, it does not always come easily. There will be times it will be hard to forgive, and we will have to intentionally make the decision to forgive over and over again. Forgiveness often does not happen overnight but takes place over time. The process is initiated by us and empowered by God. Although we can make the decision to forgive, it often takes time for the hurt and memory of an offense to fade.

There might be times when you will have to end a relationship with a person who has offended you to protect yourself. You still need to forgive that person, but forgiveness does not mean you must continue in a relationship with them—especially if they are not repentant and willing to change. God certainly does not want us to be abused. We are always to forgive but not necessarily forget. God is very concerned about our safety and sometimes the wisest thing we can do is to move on and develop more wholesome relationships.

You will know you have truly forgiven a person if when you see them, their offense is not the first thing that comes to your mind. However, if you find yourself avoiding the person who has caused an offense against you, you have not completely extended forgiveness. Do not be deceived—if you can't lovingly speak to the person who offended you, you are still holding unforgiveness in your heart and you must seek the Lord's help to forgive them. Unforgiveness left unchecked will imprison your spirit, cause bitterness, and even harden your heart. Ultimately, it will cause you to be out of the will of God. Never give anyone that kind of power over you.

My dear grandchildren, always seek to resolve relational issues quickly so no door can be opened to Satan. If an offense is resolved promptly, it will not fester or become bigger than it needs to be. Many marriages or friendships have been ruined and dissolved because of the inability to forgive. What was once something small remained unaddressed, eventually growing into something insurmountable and ugly. As Christians, we do not have the right to hold onto unforgiveness.

In my growing up years, there was a person in my life who was always at odds with different relatives and friends. It was often over silly, foolish things. This person always seemed so unhappy because they spent so much time focusing on being angry and unforgiving toward others. They had no peace in their lives and very little joy.

Christ forgave all our sins, so we must do likewise for others. If you learn to forgive quickly and willingly, you shall always be free to give and receive love. Mother Teresa, one of the most renowned saints of the twentieth century, once said, "If we really want to love we must learn how to forgive." Extend forgiveness, my dear grandchildren, and you will be healthier, happier people because of it. When we follow God's blueprint for living, our lives can be abundantly filled with His love, peace, and joy. May you always choose to forgive and be the recipient of God's forgiveness, grace, and love.

All my love,
Nana

TABLE TALK

1. How does holding
unforgiveness toward
someone hurt you more
than it hurts them?

2. What makes
unforgiveness spiritually
dangerous?

3. What actions can be
taken to help you forgive
someone who has hurt
you?

28

Learning from Others

Position yourself to learn from others so you may be wise

The way of fools seems right to them, but the wise listen to advice.
—Proverbs 12:15

As a young girl, I was brought up in a somewhat sheltered environment. When it came time to choose a college, I chose a woman's college in the city of Boston. My mom went to bat for me because my dad felt a local state college could provide the same education at a cheaper price. My mom felt the experience of meeting new people would broaden my horizons and enhance my educational experience. While in college, I became friends with many international students and I learned so much from them. There was Lemlem from Ethiopia, Assie from Ghana, Nancy from Haiti, Marlene and Sharon from Jamaica, and many more. I learned not just from what they said but more often from what they did. While others were off partying on the weekends, these young ladies were studying. They had goals and were determined to achieve them. Their diligence and discipline taught me a great deal. It is good to be exposed to people who are different than you whether that difference is in culture, religion, or financial status. The world is a big place, explore it, and learn from others.

Recipe #28: Asian Casserole (pg. 157)

My Dear Grandchildren,

At times, life can be complicated and confusing. Whether you are young or old, you will always have decisions to make—some important, some not as important. When you're young, you'll desire to grow up quickly and be your own boss. That's a good thing; it's admirable. Remember God has placed adults around you with an abundance of life experience. They are there to help and assist you. Keep in mind that no ONE person knows it all. Always remain humble and keep an open heart to learn from others.

As a little girl, my response to people who tried to help me was frequently, "I know, I know!" The message beneath those words was, "Leave me alone, I don't need your help." It was nothing but foolish pride speaking. Nannie, my mother, would correct me and say, "A person who thinks they know everything will never learn anything."

As we mature, we come to value other trusted people's opinions, experiences, and perspectives. It is only when we can see the many facets of a problem that we can make wise, godly decisions. Whenever possible, seek to be around respectable people from whom you can learn. Please know that you can "learn something from everyone" – even if it's learning what not to do. Always be open to receiving from others whom you value; your world will be expanded, and your life will be enriched.

The concept of having two parents was God's original and intentional plan. A father and mother are to bring their family up in the admonition of the Lord. They are to be God's tools to lovingly mold and shape their children. Not all children have two parents in their home. Thank God for single parents who do it alone. God surrounded the nuclear family with an extended family that consists of relatives, close friends, and church communities. They are placed there to teach, correct, and prayerfully guide us in the right direction.

Proverbs 12:15 says, "The way of fools seems right to them, but the wise listen to advice." Whenever making an important decision, first seek God. After seeking God, then seek advice from your parents and other family members who love you. Take into consideration their counsel when making your decision. By considering both God's word and your family's counsel, you will be spared making major mistakes that could affect you for a lifetime.

One of Nana's richest experiences was to attend multi-cultural churches where people came from different races, ethnicities, and backgrounds. It was so interesting to learn other individuals' perspectives on certain matters, try different types of ethnic foods, and learn various ways to do different things. My life was enriched by having those experiences. It helped me to value all people and focus on the good they possess.

Always be open to new experiences, try new things in life, and consider various options. Never be threatened by someone who is different. Learn from them. They may think differently than you but measure what they say against the truth of God's Word. There is far too much fear in the world because people feel uncomfortable with those unlike themselves. Our commonalities often outweigh our differences.

Remember, you can learn something from everyone. Praying that you will become a lifelong learner.

All my love,
Nana

TABLE TALK

1. What was the most valuable lesson you learned from another person?

2. What made that person uniquely different from other people?

3. Do you learn the most from people who are like you or are different from you?

29

Be a Good Listener

Position yourself to hear and learn by becoming an attentive
listener

To answer before listening— that is folly and shame. —Proverbs 18:13

Being an elementary school teacher for 12 years taught me a great deal. Yes, I was the teacher, but also continued to be a student. One of the more important things I learned from my students was to position yourself as close as possible to the teacher. Where you position yourself in the classroom often has a great impact on how much you learn. The students who wanted to sit in the front of the classroom were the ones who were often more motivated to listen and learn. The students who were further away from the teaching often got distracted, had shorter attention spans, and had more difficulty in listening to what was being said. When you're in a learning environment, get as close as possible to the teacher so you hear and receive all that is being taught. Desire to learn. Always be mindful that a good listener learns much. May you position yourself to be an attentive listener.

Listen! Don't stick this one in the oven! There is no baking required for this delicious cheesecake.

Recipe #29: No Bake Cheesecake (pg. 158)

My Dear Grandchildren,

An important "golden" nugget treasure for living an abundant life lies in the art of being a good listener. Always remember . . . when we speak, we speak what we already know. When we listen, we position ourselves to learn. Many a relationship, household, or friendship could be nurtured and elevated if people worked on their listening skills. Sometimes what we hear, what we interpret, and what we perceive is not at all what is actually being said. We must learn to quiet our spirits and focus on the person who is speaking. Moreover, mastering the art of listening not only serves us well in our relationships with others but also helps to strengthen our relationship with the Lord. As we learn to hear and listen to His voice in the person of the Holy Spirit, we grow in wisdom.

We live in a fast-paced world where we rush to express ourselves but are not necessarily interested in taking the time to really hear what others have to say. A spirit of pride is often in the midst of our communications. We believe that what we have to say is much more important than what the other person is saying. Instead of listening to their words, and even more importantly, their hearts, we find ourselves strategizing a rebuttal or comeback while others are still talking. Communication becomes very important in a close relationship—nothing validates and makes a person feel more loved than to be heard by their significant other. Most relationships dissolve due to one or both parties' inability to effectively communicate. Do your best to express yourself, but more importantly, be a good listener.

There are a few steps one must take in order to become a better listener. First, we must check our pride and defenses at the door of humility. Be humble and listen to what the other person is trying to express even if you don't like or agree with what you are hearing. Ask yourself, "What can I learn from them? Is there a nugget of truth I need to take and apply to myself?" Listen both with your ears and your heart. Secondly, take time to digest what is being said. Remember, we don't always need to respond with a witty rebuttal or snarky comment. Lastly, stay in the moment while listening and do not let thoughts like "when are they going to be finished?" rise up—truly hear what the other person is saying. There is an old adage that God gave us two ears and one mouth so that we'd listen twice as much as we talk.

While in conversation, let the person you are listening to know that you are present by nodding or saying, "I see." This small affirmation will create a connection between the two of you and perhaps develop an even deeper level of communication that can lead to a better relationship. If you are willing to listen, you may be pleasantly surprised by people's assessments of you. The Bible says, "Even fools are thought wise if they keep silent, and discerning if they hold their tongues." (Proverbs 17:28).

My dear grandchildren, while it is important to be a good listener to the people in our lives, it is even more important to take the time to listen to what God is speaking to us. "Listening" during my time of prayer has enhanced and strengthened my relationship with God. When most people talk about prayer, they are usually referring to their lists of petitions and requests they would like God to answer. Yes, God does hear and respond to us, but more importantly, we need to give God time to speak. It is in the quiet times when we wait and sit before God that He speaks to us in the "still small voice" of the Holy Spirit. There we receive some of His greatest treasures.

Years ago, in a church time of praise and worship, the Holy Spirit began to speak to me. I quickly sat down and began to write on the back of the church bulletin what I felt God was saying. One of the things written down was "Todd will go into ministry and become a great pastor." When reading what was written, I felt silly because it seemed so odd and unlikely. My thought was that it could not possibly come true since Grandad had a wonderful good-paying job with the phone company. Returning home after church, I placed what was written on the bulletin in the drawer of my bedside table and did not share it with Grandad because it seemed so unlikely.

About nine months later, Grandad began to share with me that he felt like God was calling him into full-time ministry. It was only then that I took out the church bulletin with the word God had spoken to me and shared it with him. Through listening and hearing the Holy Spirit that day, God not only started to prepare my heart for the big changes that were to take place in our lives but also confirmed Grandad's calling to the ministry.

Over the years, Grandad and I have made it a priority in our spiritual walks to seek God and hear what He is saying in important matters in our lives. Because we have listened and responded to God's directives, our lives have been fruitful and blessed. Remember, my dear ones, God created you and He knows the beginning from the end and sees the "whole picture" of your lives. Who better to listen to and obey? Take time on a daily basis to sit quietly before the Lord, because it will bring peace to your spirit and enable you to recognize and hear God's voice. Be determined to be a good listener and watch God move in your life.

All my love,
Nana

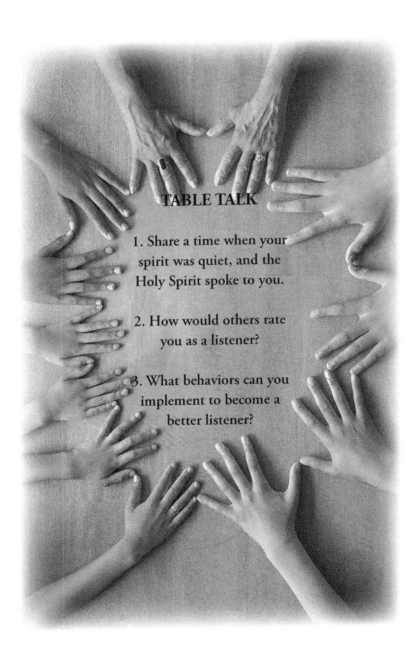

TABLE TALK

1. Share a time when your spirit was quiet, and the Holy Spirit spoke to you.

2. How would others rate you as a listener?

3. What behaviors can you implement to become a better listener?

30

Choosing a Spouse

Important considerations when choosing the right person
to marry

*Nevertheless, let each one of you in particular so love his own wife as himself,
and let the wife see that she respects her husband.* —*Ephesians 5:33*

I expected Grandad to propose to me on my 21st birthday but that didn't
happen. The day after my birthday as we sat on the couch watching TV
in Nannie and Papa's den, Grandad said, "I'm hungry. I need a snack." He
then proceeded to say, "We can have the two boxes of Cracker Jacks that
are in my car." As we sat there eating the Cracker Jacks, I came to the little
prize each box contains. I went to put it aside, but Grandad encouraged me
to open it. In opening the prize, I found a beautiful real diamond ring! It
was at that point Grandad asked me to marry him. Grandad had carefully
prepackaged my engagement ring, beforehand in order to surprise me. He
had seen someone do that on TV years before and always thought he wanted
to get engaged that way.

Regular fun and wonderful surprises are just two of the ingredients to
having a healthy marriage. A successful marriage, similar to Nana's robust pea
soup, requires several ingredients.

Recipe #30: Nana's Split Pea Soup (pg. 158)

My Dear Grandchildren,

When you get older, there will come a time when you want to settle down, commit to that one special person and marry the love of your life. May you each find the person God has ordained for you. One of the most important decisions of your life will be to choose the right person to marry. Be sure to seek the Lord's counsel in this most important matter of choosing a mate. What is often so confusing about this crucial decision is the fact that our hearts can sometimes mislead us. Beyond our hearts, we need to weigh the counsel of those who know us best, use wisdom, and most importantly, listen to the Holy Spirit.

The person you marry should love the Lord as much as you do so the two of you can walk together on a godly path. That special person God has for you should also have many of the same values your mom and dad have instilled in you. God calls us to be equally yoked. In 2 Corinthians 6:14, the Bible tells us, "Do not be yoked together with unbelievers. For what do righteousness and wickedness have in common? Or what fellowship can light have with darkness?" To be equally yoked means to be joined together with someone who holds the same values. In this case, it refers to someone who has the same basis of faith as you hold.

Always remember, God has a plan for your life and if marriage is part of that plan, it will be essential for you to have a supportive spouse. Nana feels the following are just a few of the areas that need to be considered when choosing a mate. I'm sure you will have criteria of your own. In addition to being equally yoked from a spiritual perspective, I believe the following are key considerations:

- Determine whether this person is your equal in other aspects of your life. Do they have the same family, civic, moral and educational values? I am not referring to being of the same economic class, race, or ethnicity, but to the inner values you uphold.
- Make sure this person is your very best friend and you can trust them with your heart. A strong friendship in a marriage will enable you to withstand turbulent and difficult times.

- Determine whether the two of you are willing to lay your lives down for one another's good. True love is about sacrificial giving. You will be tested and called upon to make sacrifices for the good of your marriage.
- Discern whether your life will be made better because of this person. Too often people choose a mate just because they think they can see themselves comfortably living with that person. I encourage you to find a mate you wouldn't want to live without. A mate whom you don't want to live without is someone worth loving and sacrificing for.
- Do not settle for anything less than a strong passionate love between the two of you. A strong passionate love is a love that you'll intentionally work on to keep the flame burning. Anything less than a passionate love will be smothered by life's trials.

Know, my dear ones, that even with the right mate, you'll have to be intentional in working on your marriage. No matter how perfect a fit your mate is, the two of you are still individuals coming from different life experiences. Becoming one will mean there are areas in your life that need to be changed and modified. Husbands are called to love their wives as themselves. Whether we want to admit it, we really love ourselves quite a bit. Grandsons, you should love your wives as you love yourself. Wives are called to respect their husbands, so my granddaughters, marry a man who is worthy of your respect.

Please remember that there should be an attraction to the person you marry, but you should not let looks be your determining factor. As you will soon find out—looks fade as we grow older and that can't be prevented. It is all about the beauty of the heart.

My dear ones, prayerfully at the appropriate time, you will find the love of your life and enjoy a long healthy marriage. In our family, none of us have perfect marriages but we've all determined to work at our marriages and have experienced more good times than bad. May you be blessed by the Lord to marry the person God has chosen just for you.

All my love,
Nana

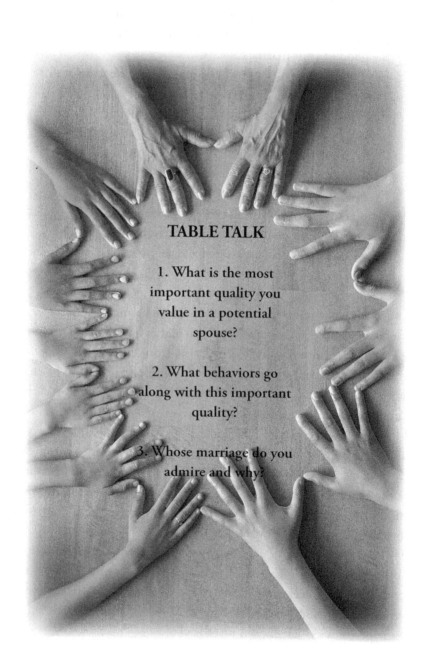

TABLE TALK

1. What is the most important quality you value in a potential spouse?

2. What behaviors go along with this important quality?

3. Whose marriage do you admire and why?

31

Creating a Legacy

Be intentional about creating your own legacy.

He decreed statutes for Jacob and established the law in Israel, which he commanded our ancestors to teach their children, so the next generation would know them, even the children yet to be born, and they in turn would tell their children.—Psalm 78:5-6

As I wrap and put a bow on this gift to you, my dear grandchildren, my prayer is that you've come to know how precious you are to us, and how deeply you are loved. This book represents my history and experiences as a legacy to pass along to each of you. It has been a labor of love to capture it for you. In the generations to come, I pray that those who come after you will have every reason to be as proud of you as I am right now. Carry on, dear ones. I thank God for you.

To those readers who are not members of my natural family, thank you for your gracious indulgence of my personal musings. I pray that your glimpses into my legacy have been a blessing. I hope you'll carry the transferable lessons forward to your own families and be encouraged to document the legacy that is uniquely your own.

Beneath the crunchy surface of my recipe for Grandad's crème brûlée is a rich creamy layer. It's what lies beneath the surface that makes it what it is, so it is with our lives. There is so much more to us than what people see on the outside. Go deep and cherish the richness that makes you who you are.

Recipe #31: Crème Brûlée (pg. 159)

My Dear Grandchildren,

The stories of our lives neither begin nor end with us. We are the product of what was and the producers of what is yet to come. Each one of us is a nexus or connecting point between the past and the future. What we inherit from previous generations is their legacy to us. What we leave for future generations is our legacy to them.

As you think about your life and all that you would like it to be, think in terms of legacy. Honor the ancestors, family, and friends who poured either directly or indirectly into your life and determine, by God's grace, to make them proud. And, if they made a positive difference in your life, they are to be commended, thanked, and appreciated while you are able to do so.

Understand that your life is never just about you. Just as others sowed into your life, you are to sow into the lives of others. You've been blessed to be a blessing to as many souls as possible. It was John Wesley, a famous preacher from the 1700's who once said, "Do all the good you can, in all the ways you can, to all the souls you can, in every place you can, at all the times you can, with all the zeal you can, as long as you can." At the end of every day, no matter how difficult or trying it may have been, think about one good thing that happened to you, and give God thanks for it. But don't stop there. Also reflect upon one good thing that you did for someone else. If you have trouble thinking of anything, pray that God gives you the next day filled with new opportunities to be a blessing. One day at a time; that's how legacies are built.

Recognize that you have both a natural heritage and a spiritual heritage. You have inherited your eye color, skin tone, and perhaps even your disposition from the DNA of your family. But more than that, if Jesus is Lord over your life, you have inherited eternal life, the Holy Spirit, and the legacy and lessons of the Holy Bible to guide you all the days of your life. The apostle John wrote, "Yet to all who did receive him, to those who believed in his name, he gave the right to become children of God— children born not of natural descent, nor of human decision or a husband's will, but born of God." (John 1:12-13)

Wow! What a legacy to have and pass along! If we put our faith in Jesus, God calls us His children. That reality, dear grandchildren, is meant to shape our destiny and legacy more than anything or anyone else.

All my love,
Nana

RECIPES

1. Banana Bread

1/2 cup Fluffo

2 eggs

2 tablespoons hot water

1/2 tsp. salt

1 cup sugar

1 3/4 cup flour

1 tsp. baking soda

3 or 4 mashed bananas

Cream sugar and Fluffo then add eggs and bananas. Then add the remaining ingredients. Bake in greased/floured loaf pan for 1 hour in a 350-degree oven.

2. Mandarin Orange Cake

Cake

1 box of yellow cake mix

4 eggs

1 – 11oz. can of mandarin oranges

1 1/2 cup vegetable oil

Frosting

1 – 9 oz. frozen whipped cream, thawed

1 – 20 oz. can crushed pineapple

1 – 3 oz. pkg. vanilla instant pudding

Combine all four cake ingredients. Mix by hand for 2 minutes. Pour batter into 3 greased and floured 8- or 9-inch round layer pans. Bake at 350 degrees for 20-25 minutes. Remove from pans to wire racks. Let cool.

Mix by hand the three ingredients for frosting well. When layers are cooled, frost between layers then do sides and top. Keep cake refrigerated.

3. Key Lime Pie IV
(Taken from online Allrecipes)

1 (9 inch) prepared Graham cracker crust or your own homemade crust

3 cups sweetened condensed milk   1/2 cup sour cream

3/4 cup key lime juice   1 tablespoon grated lime zest

Preheat oven to 350 degrees F.

In a medium bowl, combine condensed milk, sour cream, lime juice, and lime rind. Mix well and pour into graham cracker crust. Bake in preheated oven for 5-8 minutes, until tiny pinhole bubbles burst on the surface of the pie. DO NOT BROWN! Chill pie thoroughly before serving. Garnish with lime slices and whipped cream if desired.

4. Nannie's Manchup

(Cape Verdean stew-like dish)

1 1/2 lb. Pork butts, or pork chops-marinated
1 1/2 lb. Beef stew meat – marinated
2 lb. bag of yellow samp (hominy)
3 onions chopped-sautéed ahead of time
1 bunch kale (frozen or fresh) -par boiled and chopped
2 cups dry Lima beans or frozen Lima beans
3 beef bouillon cubes
2 cups dry yellow-eyed beans or shell beans
Salt to taste
Pepper to taste

Place lima beans and yellow beans in a kettle and bring to a boil then strain water to move gases. Meanwhile cook samp for 1/2 hour before adding meats, beans, onion, salt and pepper to taste. Add kale for the last hour of cooking. Add water as needed to give enough broth to the Manchup. Keep flavoring with salt and pepper when adding water. Cook until samp and beans and meat are soft. May take as long as 3-4 hours on low flame.

Some people add ketchup to flavor Manchup. Some also add butternut squash or sweet potatoes when cooking Manchup. Use your own discretion when making it. (Smile) Manchup varies from island to island.

5. Pistachio Nut Cake

Mix together with a mixer.

1 box of yellow cake mix	1/2 cup of vegetable oil
4 eggs	2 tablespoons water
1 pkg. pistachio pudding mix	1 carton (16 oz.) sour cream

Mix by hand into above mixture

1 small pkg. milk choc. chips	1/2 cup walnuts

Pour batter into oiled/floured Bundt pan. Bake 50-60 minutes in a 350-degree oven.

6. Canja
(Cape Verdean Chicken Soup with Rice)

2 tablespoons olive oil   1 large onion, chopped
5 carrots, chopped   5 celery stalks, chopped
2 dried bay leaves (whole)   1 1/2 tablespoon paprika
3 (32 oz. cartons of chicken broth)
2 lbs. boneless or reg. skinless chicken thighs
3/4 c. inexpensive white rice (not converted)
Salt and pepper to taste

In a large pot, sauté the chopped onion, carrots, and celery in the olive oil until lightly browned and softened. Next, add the chicken broth to the pot, as well as the dried bay leaves and paprika powder. Bring to a slow boil. Add the boneless, skinless chicken thighs and allow to cook on medium heat for 30-45 minutes until the chicken is fully cooked.

Next, remove the chicken thighs from the pot and cut into bite-sized pieces. Return the chicken to the pot. Add the rice (non-converted variety) to the soup. Allow the soup to simmer over low heat for 1-2 hours. The soup will thicken slightly over time as it simmers. Add salt and pepper to taste. Remove bay leaves before serving. Enjoy!

7. Marinated Carrots

2 lbs. carrots sliced (fresh or frozen)
1 can tomato soup (undiluted) 1/2 cup salad oil
3/4 cup sugar   3/4 cup cider vinegar
1 large green pepper diced   1 large onion diced
1/4 tsp. pepper   1 tsp. salt
1 tsp. prepared mustard

Slice carrots thin then cook just until crispy tender, then drain. Add all of the remaining ingredients to carrots. Let marinate in refrigerator for 24 hours. Serve cold.

8. Chicken Divan
(Nana Michelle Foster)

1 bag of frozen broccoli   2 cans of cream of mushroom soup
1 cup of mayonnaise   1 tablespoon lemon juice
3-4 boneless chicken breasts
1 1/2 tsp. curry powder or 3/4 tsp. cumin & 3/4 tsp. curry

Roll chicken in breadcrumbs and fry in margarine until browned and cooked. Cut up into one-inch pieces. Put it to one side. Boil broccoli then strain water from it. Layer broccoli on bottom of casserole dish (9x13). Place cut up fried chicken breast pieces on top of broccoli. Mix mushroom soup, mayo, lemon juice, and curry. Pour over chicken and broccoli. Sprinkle grated buttered breadcrumbs over top. Sprinkle grated cheddar cheese over breadcrumbs. Bake at 350-degree oven 3/4 - 1 hour until hot and bubbly.

9. Jag (Jagacida)
(Cape Verdean Rice and Beans)

2 cups Uncle Ben's Rice
3 tablespoons vegetable oil
2 tsp. of paprika or to taste
1 can shelled beans drained

1 large onion chopped
4 cups of water
Salt and pepper to taste

Sauté chopped onion in vegetable oil. Add water, paprika, salt, and pepper. Once boiling add beans, and rice. Cover and let simmer on low flame until done. Do not stir again.

10. Nana Lopes' Creamy Clam Chowder
(Adapted from Toll House Clam Chowder recipe)

1 1/2 inch cube of salt pork (cut in small squares)
3-4 cups of fresh or canned clam pieces
2 tablespoons butter melted   1 onion cubed and fried in salt pork
4 cups of diced potatoes   4 cups scalded whole milk
2 cans of evaporated milk   Flour in water to thicken
Salt and pepper

When the chopped onion is finished being browned with salt pork, add 2 cups of boiling water. Put in 4 cups of chopped potatoes. Boil for 5 minutes then add clams with their juice. Simmer until potatoes are done. Add milk, simmer for another 5 minutes. Add 1 pint of evaporated milk (2 cans), add melted butter, season to taste with salt and pepper. Thicken with flour and water (2 tablespoons of flour, add cold water and stir until smooth), now add to chowder.

11. Nannie's Lasagna

(Nannie Lopes' recipe)

1 lb. ground beef
1/4 tsp. garlic powder
2 cans Campbell's tomato soup
5 slices mozzarella cheese
Grated Parmesan cheese
1/2 cup water
1 pint cottage cheese or ricotta cheese

1 cup chopped onions
2 tsp. oregano
2 tsp. vinegar
1 egg mixed with cottage cheese
9 lasagna noodles cooked/drained

In sauce pan, brown beef and onion, garlic, and oregano until onion is tender. Add soup, water, and vinegar. Cook over low heat 30 minutes; stir now and then. (Add a little flour and water). In a shallow baking dish (12x8x2 inches), arrange 3 alternate layers of noodles, cottage cheese and eggs, meat sauce and mozzarella cheese. Sprinkle with Parmesan cheese. Bake at 350 degrees for 30 minutes. Let stand 20 minutes before serving.

12. Eggnog a la Jean

(Grandma Foster's recipe)

12 eggs
1 quart heavy cream
2 tsp. vanilla

1 quart milk
1 cup sugar

1. Whip 1 quart heavy cream until it forms soft peaks.
2. Beat eggs until thick.
3. Add 1/2 cup sugar gradually.
4. Add 1 quart of milk.
5. Add remaining heavy cream.
6. Add vanilla.
7. Add whipped cream.
8. Stir well and refrigerate in a covered container.

13. Cranberry Good'n Puddin

(From Ocean Spray recipe book)

1 cup fresh cranberries

1/4 cup chopped walnuts

1/2 cup sugar

1/4 cup butter melted

1/4 cup sugar

1 egg

1/2 cup flour

2 tablespoons shortening, melted

Grease well an 8" pie plate. Spread cranberries over the bottom of the plate. Sprinkle with 1/4 cup of sugar and nuts. Beat egg well. Add 1/2 cup sugar gradually and beat until thoroughly mixed. Add flour, melted butter and shortening to egg-sugar mixture. Beat well. Pour batter over top of cranberries. Bake in a slow oven at 325 degrees for 45 minutes or until crust is golden brown. Cut like pie. Serve either warm or cold with scoop of vanilla ice cream.

14. Baked Lobster Tail

(Online recipe)

4 Lobster Tails   1 stick of good quality butter
2-3 cloves of garlic   Paprika (or smoked paprika)
Old Bay   1/4 cup chopped parsley
1/2 lemon zest   1-2 tsp lemon juice
All-Purpose Seasoning (salt, pepper, garlic, onion powder)

Directions:

Preheat oven to 400 degrees. Using kitchen scissors, cut down the back of each lobster tail until right before you reach the tail. Use your fingers to dislodge the meat from the shell and set the meat on top of the shell, as seen in the video. Season Lobster adequately and place on a wire rack/baking sheet and place in the oven for 10 minutes.

Meanwhile, melt the butter and add lemon zest, juice, garlic, parsley, and seasoning. After 10 minutes in the oven, brush the melted butter mixture on the lobster tail and place in the oven on broil for 3-4 minutes or until evenly golden brown. Lobster is done at 145 degrees internal temp.

Cocktail Sauce:

1/2 cup ketchup   2-3 tablespoons horseradish
1 pinch of sugar   1 tsp. lemon juice
1 tsp Worcestershire sauce   A few dashes of hot sauce

15. Delmarva Crab Cakes

(Nana Christian's recipe)

3 tablespoons butter and 2 tablespoons onion sautéed until yellow

1 lb. crab meat	Salt and pepper to taste
1 egg beaten	1 tablespoon chopped parsley
1/2 stick butter or margarine	1 cup breadcrumbs
1 tablespoon mayonnaise	1/2 tsp. Old Bay

Lightly mix all ingredients. Shape into cakes. Brush pan with butter or margarine and fry gently.

16. Nana Christian's Apple Pie

(Nana Christian's recipe)

Crust

2 cups all-purpose flour	1 tsp. salt
3/4 cup shortening	4 to 5 tablespoons cold water

In a bowl, combine flour and salt. Cut in shortening gradually add cold water, 1 tablespoon at a time, tossing lightly with a fork until dough forms a ball. Chill for 30 minutes. On a floured surface, roll half of dough into a 10-inch circle. Place into a 9-inch pie pan.

Filling

7 to 8 cups thinly sliced peeled baking apples

2 tablespoons lemon juice	1 cup sugar
1/4 cup all-purpose flour	1 tsp. ground cinnamon
1/4 tsp. salt	1/8 tsp. ground nutmeg
1 egg yolk	1 tablespoon water
2 tablespoons butter or margarine	

Apple Filling

Toss apples with lemon juice, combine sugar, flour, cinnamon, salt, and nutmeg in a bowl. Add to apples and toss. Pour into crust, dot with butter, roll out remaining pastry to fit top of pie. Cut slits in top. Place over filling, seal and fluke edges. Beat egg yolk and water, brush over pastry. Bake at 425 degrees for 15 minutes. Reduce heat to 350 degrees, bake 40 to 45 minutes more or until crust is golden and filling is bubbly. Yields 8 servings.

17. Magic Cookie Bars

1 1/2 cup graham cracker crumbs
1 (14 oz. can) Eagle Brand Sweetened Condensed milk
1 (6 oz.) bag semi-sweet chocolate morsels
1/2 cup margarine
1 1/3 cup flaked coconut
1 cup chopped walnuts

Preheat oven to 350 degrees (325 degrees for glass dish) in a 13 x 9-inch baking pan. Melt margarine in oven in pan. Sprinkle graham crumbs over margarine. Press graham crumbs firmly down. Pour condensed milk over crumbs. Top evenly with chocolate morsels, coconut, chopped walnuts. Press down firmly. Bake 25 to 30 min. or until lightly browned. Cool thoroughly before cutting. Store loosely covered at room temperature.

18. Nana Lopes' Cream Cake
(Cream filled cake made for the infirm)

Cake Ingredients

2 eggs

1/2 cup flour

Pinch of salt

1/2 cup sugar

1/4 tsp. baking powder

Beat egg whites until stiff. Add egg yolks and beat well. Add sugar, beat again. Fold in flour with baking powder, and pinch of salt. Bake in 7-inch greased and floured pan for 33 minutes at 350-degree oven. When done cool on rack. Once cooled, slice cake into 2 thin layers.

Filling

Mix the following in a medium saucepan over a low flame. Stir until it thickens into a pudding consistency.

1 cup milk

1/4 cup sugar

1 egg

1 tablespoon flour

1 tsp. vanilla extract or lemon extract—your preference

Place filling between the 2 thin layers of the cake. Top cake with confectionery sugar. Guaranteed to make you feel better!

19. Nana Christian's Chicken Pot Pie

(Nana Christian's Recipe)

One chicken cooked and cubed
1 can cream of chicken soup   2 1/2 cups chicken broth
1 pint peas   1 pint chopped carrots, cooked
Salt and pepper to taste

Combine the above ingredients and pour into a 9x12 pan. Next follow instructions for crust.

Crust
Mix together:

1 1/2 cups of flour   2 tablespoons of baking powder
3/4 tsp. of salt   1 1/2 cups of milk
6 tablespoons of melted butter

Pour crust over chicken mixture, do not stir. Bake at 400 degrees for 30 minutes or until the crust is golden. Serves 8.

20. Sautéed Yellow Summer Squash

(Nana Christian's Recipe passed down to Nana)

4 summer squashed-washed and sliced
2 tsp. of oregano or basil (your preference)
1 medium onion- chopped   2 tablespoons olive oil
1 tsp. sugar   Salt and pepper to taste

Use covered pan. Heat oil and sauté onion until yellowed. Place squash, oregano or basil, sugar, salt and pepper. On very low flame sauté covered squash. Stir often until done. Yummy!

21. Prime Rib Roast

(Online Recipe for 10-pound boneless rib eye)

Preheat oven to 500. BUY BLUETOOTH oven thermometer, and PURCHASE OUTSIDE OVEN MEAT PROBE BLUETOOTH THERMOMETER.

Prepare Butter mix

2 sticks room temp butter | Rosemary pluck leaves and thyme
Tablespoons of garlic paste | Fold with spatula

Prepare prime rib

(Prime rib should be at room temp – can take up to 6 hours)

Rub on butter mix

Then:

Sprinkle on onion power
Sprinkle on garlic powder
Sprinkle on fresh cracked pepper
Sprinkle on smoked paprika

Roast Instructions:

Roast 3 hours 40 minutes total time – at 500 degrees for 5 minutes per pound

(500 degrees x 5 minutes per pound. = 50 minutes, we said we would add 5 minutes so 55 minutes—turn oven off for 2 hours.

Rest 30-45 minutes.

Carve bone away (save bones for rib meal).

22. Summer Jag

(Nana Pereira's recipe of rice and beans with butternut squash and kale)

1 lb. rice	1 lb. kale
1 butternut squash	1 pkg. frozen lima beans
1 quart of water	1 tsp. salt
1/2 tsp. pepper	1 tablespoon paprika

Par boil kale the day before and clean out the butternut squash—wash it and chop it up into 1-inch pieces.

Next day fry onions in oil or bacon fat until golden brown, add butternut squash and water, add salt, pepper and paprika. When water starts to boil, add the parboiled kale cut up. When water starts to boil again add rice, then add 1 pkg. frozen lima beans. When it starts to boil again, lower the flame and simmer 30 minutes until rice is cooked and water has disappeared. Do not stir.

23. Nannie's Gingersnap Cookies

(Nannie Lopes' recipe)

2 cups flour	3/4 tablespoon ginger
2 tsp. baking soda	1 tsp. cinnamon
1/2 tsp. salt	3/4 cup shortening
1 cup sugar	1 egg
1/4 cup molasses	Granulated sugar

Combine and sift dry ingredients. Add shortening, gradually add sugar, mixing until fluffy. Beat in eggs and molasses.

Form dough into small balls, roll in granulated sugar. Place 2 inches apart on ungreased cookie sheet. Bake in moderate oven 350 degrees for 12-15 minutes or until tops are slightly rounded, crackly and browned.

24. Auntie Ethel's Chocolate Torte

Crust

 1 stick margarine 1 cup flour
 1/2 cup nuts

Mix the above with a fork. With your hand pat the crust on the bottom of a 9 x 13 pan. Bake in a 350-degree oven until lightly browned. Cool.

Filling

 1 8oz. cream cheese 1 cup confectionery sugar
 1 lg. instant chocolate pudding 1 lg. container Cool Whip
 1 cup of crushed walnuts

Beat cream cheese with confectionery sugar. Fold in 1/2 container of Cool Whip. Spread over cooled crust. Mix 3 cups cold milk with Chocolate pudding mix. Spread over cream cheese mixture, then spread the rest of Cool Whip over pudding. Sprinkle with the crushed nuts.

25. Juju's Creamy Holiday Fudge
(Auntie Juju's yearly Christmas present)

 3 cups (semi-sweet) chocolate morsels
 1 can Eagle Brand sweetened condensed milk
 Dash of salt
 1 1/2 tsp. vanilla extract
 1/2 cup of chopped nuts

Melt chocolate in double broiler. Remove from heat. Add condensed milk, vanilla and nuts. Spread on waxed paper-lined 8x8 pan. Chill for 2 hours.

26. Cheese Straws

(Grandma Morris' Guyanese snack recipe)

4 sticks of butter, softened
1 tsp. mustard
1 lb. finely grated sharp cheddar cheese
Pinch cayenne pepper (optional)
1 1/4 lb. (approximately 4 1/2 cups) flour

Preheat oven to 350°F. Combine butter, cheddar cheese, mustard and a pinch of cayenne pepper (optional) and mix until smooth. Next, add flour to the cheese mixture, 1/2 cup at a time, until you achieve a soft dough like consistency (mixture should be smooth and spreadable and soft enough to be squeezed out of a pastry bag). Put the mixture into a pastry bag with a large star tip for piping. Pipe mixture into 4- to 5-inch long strips on to a non-stick baking sheet (or line a baking sheet with parchment paper). Bake for 10 to 12 minutes or until the cheese straws are slightly browned. Let cheese straws cool before removing from the baking sheet. Enjoy, great for parties.

27. Fresh Beef Brisket

4-5 lb. Fresh Brisket   1 small bottle ginger ale
1 envelope onion soup mix   1 cup ketchup

Mix together ginger ale, onion soup mix, and ketchup. Pour over brisket in covered oven pan. Bake at 375 degrees oven covered for 2 hours and uncovered for 1 hour.

28. Asian Casserole

(Nannie Lopes' Recipe)

2 cans cream of mushroom soup

2 tablespoons oil | 1 cup chopped onions
1 cup celery | 2 lbs. hamburger
1 cup uncooked rice | 1 can bean sprouts
1 can water chestnuts | 4 tablespoons soy sauce
Salt and pepper to taste | 1 pkg. frozen pea pods
1 can chow mein noodles

Put 2 tablespoons of oil in a skillet and sauté 1 cup of chopped onions and 1 cup of celery. Add 2 lbs. of hamburger and cook until browned. Add 2 undiluted cream of mushroom soup, 1 cup uncooked rice, 1 can bean sprouts (with liquid), 1 can of water chestnuts (drained and sliced). Add 4 tablespoons of soy sauce, salt and pepper to taste. If you are making this in the morning you can stop here and finish it later—if not continue in this manner. Pour into a 9 x 13 pan and bake it uncovered for 30 minutes at 350 degrees.

Then add 1 pkg. of pea pods (thawed enough to separate). Stir into above and top it all with 1 can (3 oz.) chow mein noodles. Bake it uncovered for 30 minutes at 350 degrees.

29. No Bake Cheesecake

(Nana Foster's favorite)

2 pkg. lady fingers

1-8oz. cream cheese

1 pint whipping cream

1 tsp. vanilla extract

1 can cherry pie filling

1-3oz. cream cheese

3/4 cup sugar

Line bottom and sides of cake pan with lady fingers. Whip cream cheese until it looks like whipped cream. Add sugar and vanilla. Fold whipped cream (that has been whipped) into cheese. Pour 1/2 mix into finger-lined pan. Lay more lady fingers over this then add the other 1/2 mixture over lady fingers. Top with cherry filling. Keep refrigerated until ready to eat.

30. Nana's Split Pea Soup

2 medium potatoes-chopped into 1 in. pieces

1 lb. dry green split peas

1 ham steak or ham bone

1 tablespoon chopped garlic

2 chicken bouillon

1 tablespoon olive oil

1 medium onion chopped

2 medium carrots diced

1 1/2 tsp. curry powder or cumin

Sort and rinse peas. Heat oil in a 6-to-8-quart pot. Add onion, garlic, carrots to pot. Add ham and cook for 5 minutes. Add 6 cups of water, bouillon, peas and bring water to a boil. Reduce heat, cover and simmer until peas are tender. Stir occasionally. Season with curry or cumin, salt and pepper to taste. Add more water if necessary. Season to taste again. Serves 6.

31. Crème Brûlée
(Online Recipe)

6 tbsp white sugar, (4 tbsp for custard, 2 tbsp for caramelize top)

6 egg yolks

2 1/2 cups heavy cream

1/2 teaspoon vanilla extract

2 tablespoons brown sugar

Preheat the oven to 300 degrees

1. Make the custard:
Whisk the egg yolks, sugar, and vanilla in a bowl. Heat the cream until it's almost boiling, then whisk the cream into the egg mixture. Pour the mixture into a double boiler and stir over simmering water until thick. Make sure to add the hot cream to the eggs really slowly so that they don't cook.

2. Bake and chill the custard:
Pour the mixture into crème brûlée dishes or ramekins. Bake in a preheated oven until set. Cool to room temperature, then chill in the fridge. Caramelize the sugar: Sprinkle each custard with a blend of brown and white sugars. Place under your oven's broiler until the sugar is melted and caramelized. Chill before serving.

Made with...

love

Biography

Leslie Lopes Foster was brought up in the small coastal town of Fairhaven, Massachusetts. Her immediate and extended Cape Verdean family provided a strong support system throughout her growing years. At the age of sixteen, she came into a personal relationship with Jesus Christ, a decision that forever changed the trajectory of her life. This one decision provided a world of new opportunities and possibilities for this small-town girl.

Leslie currently resides in Connecticut. She is the mother of three grown children and eight grandchildren who are the joy of her life. She has been married to her college sweetheart, Pastor Todd C. Foster for nearly 46 years. Leslie worked as an inner-city elementary school teacher for 12 years and then as a full-time inner-city associate pastor for 18 years. It was through the medley of teaching and pastoring that a passion and heart for young people was birthed. Her experience in both education and ministry has given her intimate insight into families and made her acutely aware of the parenting needs of children and youth. Her Christian-based discipleship book is meant to bring families with teenagers into conversations that will be both life-giving and instructional.

Made in United States
North Haven, CT
30 January 2024

48117577R00098